Needlecraft

Needlecraft

Jane McMorland Hunter

with Louise Carpenter

teach
yourself

To my mother,
and also to John and Lily

For UK order enquiries: please contact Bookpoint Ltd.,
130 Milton Park, Abingdon, Oxon OX14 4SB.
Telephone: +44 (0) 1235 827720. Fax: +44 (0) 1235 400454.
Lines are open 09.00–18.00, Monday to Saturday,
with a 24-hour message answering service.
You can also order through our webssite www.madaboutbooks.com

For USA order enquiries: please contact
McGraw-Hill Customer Services, PO Box 545, Blacklick,
OH 43004-0545, USA.
Telephone: 1-800-722-4726. Fax: 1-614-755-5645.

For Canada order enquiries: please contact
McGraw-Hill Ryerson Ltd., 300 Water St, Whitby,
Ontario L1N 9B6, Canada.
Telephone: 905 430 5000. Fax: 905 430 5020.

Long renowned as the authoritative source for self-guided learning –
with more than 30 million copies sold worldwide – the *Teach Yourself*
series includes over 300 titles in the fields of languages, crafts,
hobbies, business, computing and education.

British Library Cataloguing in Publication Data
A catalogue record for this title is available from The British Library.

Library of Congress Catalog Card Number: On file.

First published in UK 2000 by Hodder Headline Ltd,
338 Euston Road, London NW1 3BH

First published in US 2000 by Contemporary Books,
a Division of The McGraw-Hill Companies,
1 Prudential Plaza, 130 East Randolph Street,
Chicago, IL 60601 USA.

The 'Teach Yourself' name is a registered trade mark of
Hodder & Stoughton Ltd.

Typeset by Dorchester Typesetting Group Ltd.
Printed in Dubai for Hodder & Stoughton Educational,
a division of Hodder Headline Ltd., 338 Euston Road,
London NW1 3BH.

Impression number 10 9 8 7 6 5 4 3 2 1
Year   2009 2008 2007 2006 2005 2004 2003

Contents

Acknowledgements

Firstly I would like to thank Martin Higgs, who gave me the initial encouragement I needed to start writing in the first place. Great thanks are due to my agent, Teresa Chris, who has been a never-ending source of enthusiasm and support. Helen Green at Hodder & Stoughton has helped me along the way and has patiently dealt with all my queries, however ludicrous. I greatly appreciate the time and trouble that the design team – especially Alison Bond, Amanda Hawkes and Lee-May Lim – have taken over the appearance of the book and the skill of Steve Tanner in taking the superb photographs. I am immensely grateful to my group of stitchers – Julie Apps, Sarah Bowman, Christopher Josiffe, Toby Piachaud and Caroline Tarring – for the hours they spent as guinea-pigs testing my instructions. Barry Delves, David Piachaud and Karin Scherer have all been very helpful and encouraging in different ways. Lastly my greatest thanks are to Louise Carpenter for making sense of my garbled English and for providing the necessary support without which I would never have written this book.

Introduction

This book covers the basic aspects of the four main areas of needlecraft: embroidery, cross stitch, needlepoint and Bargello or Florentine work. The instructions are simple enough for a complete beginner to be able to master their chosen craft. Hints, tips and more advanced ideas for the more proficient stitcher are also included. All the necessary equipment is clearly explained, and the wide range of different materials available is considered. Illustrations of stitches and finished examples make everything easy to understand.

The first technique covered is embroidery, which to many people is the ultimate needlecraft. Clear illustration makes even the most complicated stitch easy. This chapter also illustrates the different effects that can be achieved by altering the yarn or fabric and shows how designs can be transferred onto the fabric.

Cross stitch is often regarded as a type of embroidery but has been given a separate chapter as the techniques and end products differ. It is a fairly simple, and deservedly popular, form of embroidery and beautiful effects can be created comparatively easily.

There are two chapters devoted to needlepoint. Many people master basic techniques such as tent stitch and cross stitch, but never progress further. Together, these two chapters show how different effects can be achieved by varying the stitch and adding more complicated ones, and by mixing colours and changing the canvas.

Bargello or Florentine work involves techniques that have deep historical roots and have found a new popularity in recent years. Detailed instructions on working the stitches, and the variations possible, are included in the chapter on Bargello.

Each chapter includes projects, which are easy to undertake once you've mastered the stitches. You will soon find yourself making beautiful and unusual objects from around the world!

Basic equipment

This chapter tells you about any equipment you may need while learning the various techniques described. Don't be put off if you read through and find you do not possess any of the items. Some things, such as the correct needles, are vital, but in other cases what you have to hand may substitute perfectly well – for example, dressmaking scissors are undoubtedly useful but to begin with ordinary scissors will probably do just as well and an old school ruler could easily serve as a tape measure. Whatever you do, don't rush out and buy masses of things you may never use, however tempting they may look in the shop! Buy what you require for the particular project you are working on and gradually you will build up a collection of the equipment *you* need.

■ Types of threads: stranded cotton, pearl cotton, matte embroidery cotton, crewel yarn, Persian yarn, tapestry wool, metallic thread.

Yarns and threads

Yarns and threads are used to create the pattern on the fabric: yarn usually referring to wool and thread referring to cotton, silk or synthetic fibre. Yarns and threads are made up of strands and plies. A strand is a single unit, which is made up of a number of plies. Strands are easily separated but plies are not.

The yarns and threads suitable for needlecraft vary enormously, but one important factor is that they should remain uniform throughout their length. Uneven yarns, which can be used in knitting, are rarely used in needlecraft as they do not easily pass through the fabric. For the same reason, always try to use good-quality yarn or thread as this will tend to be more even and therefore easier to work with. Any irregularities in the thread tend to be magnified when it has been passed through the fabric several times.

■ Yarns and threads come in a variety of strands and plies. Strands can be easily separated, but plies cannot.

Types of yarn and thread

A great variety of yarns and threads is available, as can be seen from the photograph opposite page 1 and the chart below.

Embroidery floss or stranded cotton
This is loosely twisted and consists of six strands of thread, which are easily divided and can be mixed according to the effect desired. It is usually made of cotton but can be silk or rayon.

Pearl cotton
This consists of two threads, tightly twisted. It is glossy and comes in a good variety of colours.

Matte embroidery cotton
This is loosely twisted and consists of five strands which can be separated and mixed in a similar way to embroidery floss. It gives the work a muted appearance and is usually used on heavier fabrics. It is also called soft cotton.

Crewel yarn
This is fine two-ply wool which is equal in thickness to one strand of Persian yarn. The two strands it is made up of can be separate or mixed.

Persian yarn
This consists of three strands of wool which are lightly twisted. Each strand is two-ply and, as with crewel yarn, the strands can be mixed to create different thicknesses or colour shades.

Tapestry wool
This is tightly twisted four-ply yarn. The individual threads cannot be separated, but more than one strand can be used to create larger stitches.

Knitting wool
This comes in a variety of thicknesses from two-ply upwards. It is not usually suitable for needlework as the colour range can be limited and the quality sometimes erratic.

Metallic threads
These come in a great variety of thicknesses but are usually only used in small quantities for special effects. They tend to be more difficult to work with and many are not hardwearing.

How thread is supplied

Threads and yarns come in various quantities, usually described as skeins (small) and hanks (large). The sizes vary according to the manufacturer. Obviously it is cheaper to buy in hanks if you require a lot of a certain colour, but be careful as it is very easy to end up with large quantities of colours you are unlikely to use again. Colours vary between manufacturers and, although the cottons are fairly uniform, the wools themselves vary considerably. Anchor is the fluffiest and DMC the thickest. Many people have personal preferences, but for most projects Appleton wool is a good choice as it comes in a wide range of colours and does not tend to knot or snag. It is important not to mix different brands within one project as the work will look uneven.

Types of yarn and thread

Thread type	Brand	Skein	Hank
Tapestry	Appleton	11 yds/10 m	60 yds/55 m
Tapestry	DMC	8.8 yds/8 m	42.7 yds/39 m
Tapestry	Anchor	11 yds/10 m	110 yds/100 m
Crewel	Appleton	27.5 yds/25 m	192 yds/175 m
Crewel	DMC Medici	27.5 yds/25 m	192 yds/175 m
Persian	Paterna	8 yds/7.3 m	40 yds/37 m
Stranded	Anchor	8.8 yds/8 m	
cotton	DMC	8.8 yds/8 m	
	Madeira	11 yds/10 m	
Pearl cotton	DMC	27.5 yds/25 m	
	Anchor	25 yds/22 m	
Matte/soft	Anchor	11 yds/10 m	
cotton	DMC	11 yds/10 m	

Fabric and canvas

Most fabrics and canvases for needlecraft are made of cotton or linen and come in a variety of types and thread counts. This is often written or referred to as the gauge or mesh of the material. The thread count determines the size of each stitch and is therefore very important in determining the size and appearance of the finished piece. The thread count is the number of threads in a 1" (2.5 cm) length. Canvases can come in anything from 18# (18 stitches per inch or 2.5 cm) to 3# (3 stitches per inch or 2.5 cm) and fabrics as fine as 32# can be bought. The finer counts take far longer to stitch, but allow a much more detailed design. Large thread counts such as 7# or 5# use more than one strand of tapestry wool and are therefore thicker, which makes them suitable for rugs and tablecloths. These large thread counts grow quickly but are probably not suitable for a first-time stitcher as they can easily distort if the stitches are not uniform in tension.

Embroidery fabric

Virtually any fabric can be used for embroidery, from the finest silk or muslin down to heavy wools or felt. Many fabrics are produced specifically for needlecraft and in most cases these are the easiest to use. If you do choose other fabrics to work on remember to avoid anything knitted or stretchy as your stitches will not lie flat on it. The suitable fabrics fall into three main categories.

Even-weave

With this fabric, the number of threads in any area is the same for the warp and weft – there are the same number of vertical and horizontal threads. This makes counting easy and produces uniform-sized stitches. Several fabrics in this category are produced specifically for cross stitch, Aida and Binca being two of the most well known. Aida comes in a good range of colours and in sizes 18# to 11#, whereas Binca is usually 6# and comes in a smaller range of brighter colours. Binca is particularly popular with children.

■ Fabrics for needlecraft include Aida, plain weave, printed cotton, canvas (both single and double).

Before you choose a fabric, make sure you will enjoy working on it – fine embroidery on 32# linen may look beautiful, but it will be fiddly to stitch and will probably only suit you if you are patient and have plenty of time to spare and good eyesight. On the other hand, 14# Aida is very easy to use and you will find that your design grows quickly for comparatively little effort. Neither method is better than the other, but you should consider what type of sewing you would enjoy before embarking on a project.

Most even-weaves are linen or linen and cotton mix, and, although they may seem expensive, for many projects you will need only a small piece. As with the threads, always try to buy good-quality fabric. Many shops sell small off-cuts or remnants and these can be very reasonably priced.

Plain weave

This is the fabric you are most likely to meet in non-specialist shops. It is usually closely woven, has a smooth surface and can be suitable for embroidery. The thing to be wary of is that the warp and weft threads are not always even – in other words you will not be able to count the threads to produce an even design. This makes it more suitable for freestyle embroidery than counted work such as cross stitch.

Regular patterns

Some plain weaves have a surface pattern, which makes it possible to use them for counted work. Gingham is particularly suitable for this, as is fabric with stripes or a regular pattern of dots. Make sure the design really *is* regular and that the fabric itself is firm enough to support the stitches. Cotton is usually the most suitable, although silks and damask can also be used. Again, make sure the fabric is not stretchy.

Canvas

Apart from the different gauge sizes, canvases are also available in a number of types. The most common are plain single or interlocking. These both appear to be made up of single threads, but only in plain (or single mesh) is the canvas formed by the intersection of single horizontal and vertical threads. Interlocking canvas appears to be made up of single threads but in fact each of the verticals is actually two threads intertwined. This results in a canvas that distorts very little and is easy to count stitches on – a very important factor when working from a chart.

Double or Penelope canvas

This consists of double rows of horizontal and vertical threads. The advantages are that the canvas is very strong and that the stitch size can be varied within the piece. This is useful if the design calls for a finely stitched area. The gauge is given as two numbers – for example, 10/20 would mean that if the threads were sewn in pairs there would be ten stitches per inch (2.5 cm) and that if each thread were stitched individually there would be twenty stitches over the same area.

Rug canvas

This consists of interlocking threads, both horizontally and vertically. It comes in 3# to 5# and, as its name implies, is primarily used for making rugs.

Plastic or synthetic canvas

This type of canvas is moulded rather than woven. It is very stiff and usually only comes in large gauges.

Paper canvas

Paper canvas can be used for making cards, bookmarks or pictures.

Waste canvas

This is a loosely woven canvas which comes in a variety of gauges. You can tack it onto any firm fabric so that it provides an even set of vertical and horizontal threads which you can use for counting. When you have finished stitching, you can gently pull the threads of waste canvas away using tweezers.

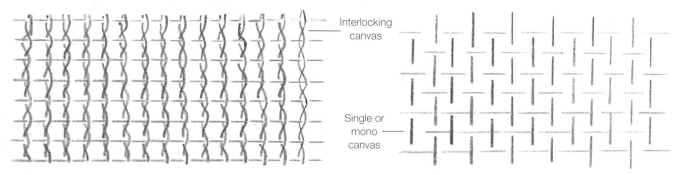

Interlocking canvas

Single or mono canvas

■ An interlocking canvas (left) distorts less when working than a single canvas, and is easy to count stitches on.

Needles

Needlecraft uses three main types of needle – crewel, chenille and tapestry. Each comes in a range of sizes – the larger the number, the shorter and finer the needle. The type and size of needle you use will be dictated by the technique and thread you are using. It is important that the needle should pass through the fabric easily and not be so small that it causes the thread to fray.

- Crewel needles are medium-length needles with sharp points which are available in sizes 1 to 10. They are used for most embroidery.
- Chenille needles also have sharp points, but are longer and thicker with larger eyes. They come in sizes 14–26 (not on the same scale as crewel) and are used for embroidering with heavy threads.
- Tapestry needles are similar to chenille needles and come in the same sizes, but have blunt ends. This makes them most suitable for canvas work as they will not pierce the threads.

Gold-plated needles are available in most sizes and, although they may seem expensive, they are much easier to work with.

Frames

Many types of needlecraft can be hand held, but some need the extra support of a frame to stop the fabric distorting. Frames come in various types, but these can be divided into three main groups.

Hoops

Hoops consist of two wooden rings which fit inside each other. The outer hoop is adjustable, allowing the fabric to pass between the two hoops. Once the outer hoop is tightened, the fabric enclosed in the ring will be held tight.

Hoops come in a variety of sizes and are convenient to use, but can seriously distort the fabric. They should not be left on the fabric when you are not stitching and should *only* be used on fine fabric where any distortion can be ironed out. Tempting as these may seem, rectangular frames should be used wherever possible as they do not mark the fabric.

Rectangular frames

These consist of an adjustable wooden rectangle onto which the fabric is attached. The top and bottom rods have a strip of tape fixed to them to which the top and bottom of the canvas should be firmly stitched. The rods are fixed to side poles which consist of adjustable metal screws or wooden batons which allow the poles to rotate. This means that any unused portion of canvas can be wound round the poles.

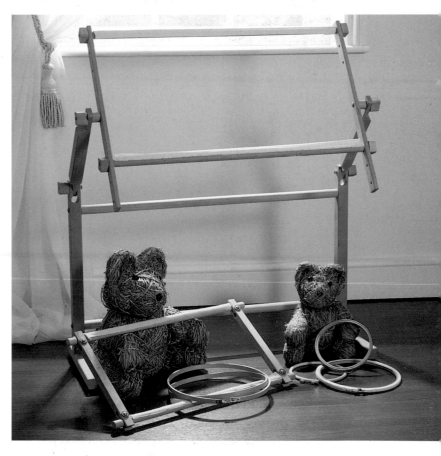

■ Using a frame can help to keep your work from distorting.

Rectangular frames come in a variety of sizes and some come with a floor stand, which has the advantage of freeing both hands but the disadvantage of not being portable. The horizontal poles must be slightly longer than the width of the fabric, but the frames are surprisingly easy to manage as all the unused canvas is wound away.

Stretcher frames

These consist of two pairs of stretchers which slot together, but they can be unwieldy for large projects as the stretcher frame must be large enough to accommodate the entire canvas.

The canvas should not be removed from rectangular or stretcher frames until the work is finished.

Accessories

Dressmaking scissors

These are large scissors which are useful for cutting canvas or fabric. The handles are usually different sizes to allow you to put more than one finger in, thus allowing for greater accuracy. Dressmaking scissors should *never* be used for cutting paper because this blunts them.

Embroidery scissors

These are small scissors with sharp pointed ends. They are useful for cutting threads and trimming work.

■ Some of the accessories that are useful in needlecraft.

Pinking shears

For most people these will be a luxury rather than a necessity, but they can be used to create interesting effects. They are similar to ordinary dressmaking scissors, but have thick indented blades which result in a zig-zag cut.

Binding tape

Tape is used to cover the raw edges of canvas to stop it fraying. Fine fabrics can be hem-stitched to avoid fraying, but many thicker fabrics and all canvases need to be bound at the edges. How to do this is explained in each section. Binding stops the fabric from fraying and also covers any rough edges of canvas which could damage the yarn. It is possible to use masking tape, but this is not as hardwearing and can become sticky.

Tape measure

This should be soft and flexible. Most tape measures are 1.5 m long and are marked in both inches and centimetres.

Thimbles

A thimble fits on the middle finger of the hand in which you hold the needle. They are made of metal or plastic and come in a variety of sizes. They are not necessary when using tapestry needles, but provide useful protection when stitching with finer, sharper crewel needles. They take a certain amount of getting used to and it is important to have one that fits your finger exactly. For this reason the more expensive metal thimbles tend to be better value as they will bend to the shape of your finger.

Needle threader

This is a simple metal device which makes threading needles easy. It is particularly useful when using crewel wool, which tends to be fluffy. However, if you are stitching with tapestry wool you will probably never need one.

Cotton thread

Ordinary dressmaking thread is needed for hemming or binding the edge of the fabric or canvas and for finishing off the project. Always use the same type of thread as the fabric – for example, synthetic thread on artificial fibres and cotton on natural fabrics such as cotton or linen. Thread is also useful for tacking shapes onto the fabric or canvas – for example, the edge of the pattern or where the design changes.

Designing patterns

A number of items, though not essential, will make the work of designing patterns much easier.

Squared paper

This is invaluable if you want to create your own designs for needlepoint, cross stitch or Bargello. It comes in a variety of sizes and it is a matter of personal preference which you choose.

Tracing paper

This is useful for embroidery if you wish to copy designs from books as you can then transfer the design directly onto the fabric.

Pens and crayons

Felt-tip pens can be used for designing, but crayons tend to be better as they usually come in a wider range of colours and can be rubbed out if you make a mistake or change your mind.

Waterproof pens and dressmaking pencils

These are permanent and can be used to mark the fabric, providing the marks will be stitched over. A great many specialised markers are available: these are fully discussed in the chapter on embroidery.

Charts and diagrams

The methods of designing patterns for embroidery, cross stitch, needlepoint and Bargello vary considerably and each is discussed in detail in the relevant chapter. However, some basic comparisons will be useful to help you select the correct technique for the pattern you have chosen or vice versa.

If you are working from a kit, the method will have been determined for you and it is likely that the design will have been printed on the fabric. If this is the case all you have to do is stitch over the relevant coloured areas. This may seem the easiest method, but for cross stitch, needlepoint and Bargello working from a chart is much more accurate and, once you have got used to the technique, much simpler.

Designs for embroidery need to be marked directly onto the fabric. Almost any design can be worked in embroidery because there is such a wide variety of stitches available. Designs from books are particularly

easy to adapt as all you have to do is trace the original and then transfer it onto the fabric. How to do this is explained fully in the chapter on embroidery. Copying other pieces of embroidery can be more difficult as you need to be able to draw the design freehand onto the fabric without the help of a tracing. Before you choose the design it is important to bear in mind which stitches would be suitable and how much detail you wish to include.

The photograph shows how different the same design can look worked in different stitches. Although the finished results look very different, the design method for needlepoint and cross stitch is identical. The pattern is worked from a chart on squared paper, with each square on the chart representing one stitch on the fabric or canvas. Before you start to stitch, you must transfer the design or picture you have chosen onto the squared paper. It is important to remember that because of the nature of the stitches (cross stitch or wool on canvas) it is not particularly easy to stitch fine curves. If you have chosen a design which involves a lot of detailed curved work, it may be better to stitch it in embroidery.

Bargello is also worked from a chart, with the lines on the paper representing the threads of the canvas. All designs in Bargello consist of vertical stitches placed next to each other in a series of steps. The pattern is formed by a combination of the size of the stitch, the steps between each stitch and the colour used. Because of this, geometric patterns are the most suitable for Bargello work. A single pattern is repeated across the canvas, with variations in colour creating the overall design.

■ The same design can look very different when worked in different stitches.

■ Charts are used to design patterns in cross stitch, needlepoint and Bargello work.

Chart for needlepoint and cross stitch

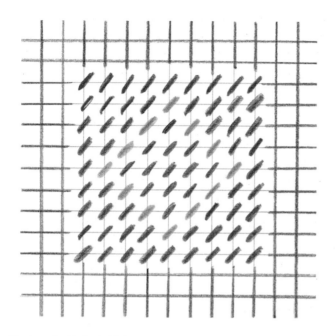

Chart worked in tent stitch

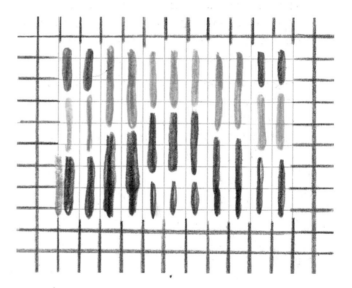

Bargello stitches

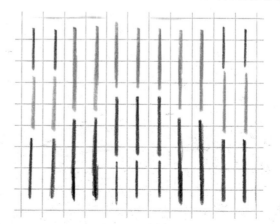

Bargello chart

Chart worked in cross stitch

2

Embroidery

Embroidery is, without doubt, the most versatile type of needlecraft. Any type of thread – silk, cotton, wool, metallic or string – can be stitched onto any fabric, from leather and thick woollen blankets down to the finest gauze. To extend the range of possibilities even further an enormous variety of objects can then be stitched on. In various parts of the world and at various times in history feathers, bones, shells, buttons, beads, tassels and mirrors have all been used in embroidery.

It is impossible to tell exactly where and when embroidery originated as very few early examples have survived. The Chinese believe the wife of the Emperor Yao founded embroidery sometime in the third millennium BC, whereas in Europe Minerva, the goddess of handicrafts, is credited with its invention. Pieces have been found in Egypt in the tombs of Tuthmosis IV (1401–1391 BC) and Tutankhamum (1333–1323 BC) and some ancient pieces have been found in China. Unfortunately, Chinese embroideries are difficult to date accurately because the designs were highly symbolic and changed very little in over 2000 years. The problem is similar in India, where the Code of Manu laid down strict rules for the design and production of embroidery which are still partially adhered to, even though the code was issued over 2500 years ago.

The first well documented use of embroidery is by the Greeks and Romans, who had their togas decorated with gold thread from Phrygia on the Aegean.

The next oldest famous piece of embroidery is the Bayeux Tapestry, which depicts the invasion of England by William the Conqueror in 1066. Its title is in fact incorrect, as it is not woven tapestry but linen with woollen stitches.

In medieval times, England became renowned throughout Europe for the production of *Opus Anglicanum* – very fine stitched work with silver threads, seed pearls and semi-precious stones. Produced by professionals mostly working in London, it was sought by rulers and church dignitaries and as a result many examples have been preserved.

Until the late eighteenth century in Europe and North America embroidery for pleasure was the preserve of the rich, who had both the time and the money to indulge themselves. Pieces were also made for the church, but for most people stitching was a necessity and most of the beautiful pieces that have survived were produced to display a skill rather than just for pleasure.

Throughout the nineteenth century in Europe this began to change gradually and at the end of the century 'Art Needlework' was introduced by William Morris. It was part of a general reaction against industrialisation that was gaining ground at the time and the fine, delicately embroidered designs soon became widespread. Earlier in the century Berlin woolwork had become popular because it was so easy; here the reverse was true – Art Needlework caught on because its difficulty and fineness was felt to make it exclusive.

In the twentieth century there was another great revolution with the invention of machine embroidery. At first many people refused to accept it as real embroidery, regarding it simply as a poor imitation. Gradually, however, it has gained ground and is now as popular as hand stitching. The techniques are very different; and machine embroidery is not covered in this book.

In much of Europe and North America embroidery is regarded as a pastime for women with free time, but in other parts of the world the picture could not be more different. Even though many people are unaware of the symbolism involved, a great many designs are handed down through the generations in places like Central Asia, China and India and, although the patterns *do* alter, they tend to change less than in the West where mass-produced patterns simply cater for the latest fashion. Objects used to decorate embroidery are also very important. For example, cowrie shells have always been regarded as powerful protectors and mirrors are believed to avert the evil eye. Sequins were particularly popular, especially in Europe where their sparkle led them to be associated with rulers and great wealth.

Embroidery is popular throughout the world today, with examples ranging from mass-produced kits to fine church robes or tribal talismans.

Equipment

As explained in Chapter 1, there is a huge range of fabrics which can be used for embroidery. The projects here all use linen or linen and cotton mix as they are easy to stitch on and are hardwearing. Before you choose a fabric, make sure that it is suitable for the finished object you have in mind, and for the type of stitches you wish to use. As a general rule, very fine stitches look better on fine fabrics, whereas larger, chunkier work is more suited to felts or woollen blankets.

The threads you can use for embroidery are also described in Chapter 1. The projects here use crewel wool, stranded cotton and matte or soft cotton, which all produce quite different effects. Do not be afraid to experiment – for example, fluffy wool, such as mohair, would contrast well with silky pearl cotton. As with all experiments, test your ideas out on a small piece of fabric first – if you do not plan the use of threads well it can look as if you are using up the contents of an old workbasket! A safe guideline to follow is that thick thread will stand out more in terms of design, but will lose the finer detail possible with a more delicate thread.

For nearly all embroidery the easiest needle to use is a crewel needle. It is particularly important to use the correct size as the fabric used for embroidery can often distort if you use a needle that is too large and the thread will fray if it is too small.

As with the other techniques, whether or not you use a frame is often a matter of personal preference. With some embroidery stitches, however, a frame is a necessity – for example, satin stitch can easily cause the fabric to pull and distort.

Designs

Before you can start to stitch, you need to choose a design and mark it on the fabric. You can do this in a number of ways, which are explained below. Be careful to choose a picture or design that will be suitable for the materials you are working with.

Ready printed

Many pieces of embroidery fabric can be bought with the design already printed for you. This is obviously the easiest choice but the designs can be very limiting.

Freehand drawing

With this method you draw directly onto the fabric with a specialist pen. These pens can be found in all needlecraft shops and come in a wide range. Some are water soluble and can be washed out after you have finished stitching; others are permanent and need to be stitched over exactly. A third type is those which fade, usually over a specified period like two hours. They seem ideal, but unless you are stitching a small area it is very irritating to see your design fade away before you have finished it and then have to redraw it.

Drawing freehand on fabric may sound intimidating, but is no more difficult than drawing on paper. Always try the drawing out on a sheet of paper first to check for size and suitability. Another method is to make a template of card and draw round it – this is the method used in both the Dragon project and the Elizabethan Flower project further on in this chapter. Do not be tempted to draw with anything other than a specialist pen: many felt-tips and lead pencils dirty the threads.

Iron-on transfers

These can come with ready-drawn designs or you can make your own. Specialist needlecraft shops sell a particular type of waxy pen for this purpose and you simply use it to draw your design onto tracing paper. To print the transfer onto the fabric, just place it face downwards and press firmly using a hot iron.

(Manufacturers' instructions vary slightly so always read them carefully first.) This method is simple to use, but has the disadvantage that the design is reversed when it is placed on the fabric. This obviously doesn't matter for many designs, but would not be suitable for anything involving lettering.

Dressmaker's carbon

This is the method many people find most satisfactory. The paper is similar to typing carbon, but do not be tempted to use this as it smudges. Dressmaker's carbon comes in light and dark and you should buy whichever is most suitable for the fabric you are using – dark-coloured carbon should be used on light fabrics as it will show up better.

If you are using this method you *must* transfer the whole design in one go because it is extremely difficult to line up part of the pattern at a later stage. It is really only suitable for smooth fabrics, which should be pressed first. Lay the fabric on a firm, flat surface and then place the carbon paper on top of it, shiny side down. If necessary, secure both fabric and carbon with masking tape. Then place the design you have chosen on top of the carbon and tape it in place. Draw over the design, pressing firmly but taking care not to smudge your outlines – you need to hold your hand above the paper rather than resting on it as the carbon could mark your fabric. You can buy tracing wheels specifically for this, but with a little practice you will get just as good results using a ball-point pen.

As with everything else, try it out on a piece of spare fabric first. When you have finished the drawing, remove the carbon paper and you will find that the pressure on the carbon has transferred the design onto the fabric. When you stitch, try to cover the carbon marks; if any remain, simply wash them out gently at the end.

Tracing onto the fabric

This is only possible with very fine fabric such as muslin or gauze. Simply place the fabric over the design, tape it firmly in place and trace the design showing through. As before, use only specialist pens for this.

Tissue paper and tacking

This method is most suitable for highly textured fabrics such as tweeds, where pen or transfer lines would not show up clearly. First trace the design onto tissue paper, then place the paper over the fabric and tack or tape it firmly down. Using small tacking stitches, follow the lines of the design. When you have stitched all the design, you can gently tear away the tissue paper, leaving the design outlined on the fabric. You can either embroider over the tacking stitches to hide them or pull them out at the end.

Pricking and pouncing

This is a very traditional method of transferring designs and is suitable for any smooth fabric. First you need to punch holes along the outline of the design. Place the original on a drawing board or thick wad of fabric and punch holes all along using a thick pin or needle. If you have a sewing machine you can use this to create the holes by removing the thread and putting it on a fairly large stitch setting. Be careful to prick the holes close enough together to let all the details show through. Lay the pricked design on the fabric and secure with pins. Using a small pad of felt rub pounce into the holes (this is a type of powdered dressmaker's chalk and is available from needlecraft shops). Remove the paper, blow away any excess pounce and join up the dots on the fabric. Again, always use a specialist pen for this.

Which of the above methods you use may be determined by the design and fabric you have chosen: if not, try the various techniques and see which you prefer. For many projects it comes down to personal preference. I always try to draw directly onto the fabric or use templates but many people find using dressmaker's carbon easier.

Enlarging or reducing designs

It is unlikely that the design you have chosen will be exactly the size for the project you have in mind. If you need to alter the original you can either reduce or enlarge it on a photocopier or use a grid. To do this you need to draw an accurate grid over the original. Make sure you place the lines close enough together so you can easily copy the shapes within each square (1" (2.5 cm) is usually a good distance). Then count the squares and draw a grid the correct size for your project – for example, if you needed to double the size of the original, each square would now be 2" (5 cm) square. It is then easy to enlarge or reduce the original by copying each square onto the new grid.

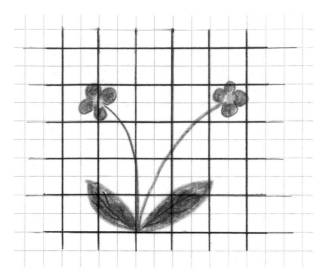

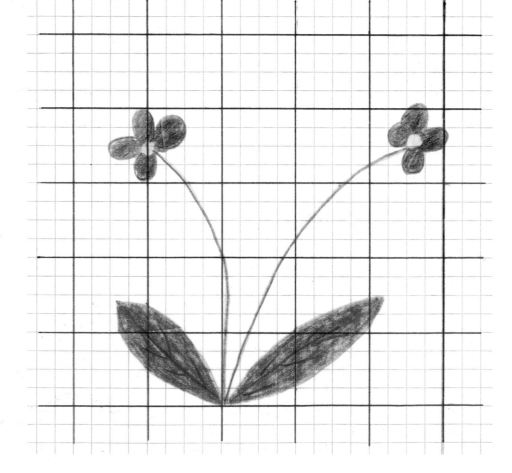

■ Enlarging and reducing designs using a grid.

Starting

The threads you sew with should be no longer than 30" (75 cm). This may seem to involve a lot of casting on and off, but if you use longer lengths the thread will tend to knot and become uneven.

For some projects you will need to separate the strands of the thread. To do this, cut the correct length of thread, divide it as required and then hold one group of threads in your mouth. Pulling the other group of threads away gently, let the original thread untwist in your other hand. Do not pull too quickly or the thread will become very twisted.

Before you start stitching you will need to protect the edges of your fabric, either by folding the edges over or by binding them with tape. Make sure you leave enough space round your design to complete the project – for example, if you are making a tablemat, the fabric needs to be large enough for the size of the finished mat, not just large enough to accommodate your design. If you are using binding tape, place it over the edge of the fabric so half is above and half below. Then tack round, ensuring both sides of tape are attached to the fabric. Fold the tape over at an angle at the corners to ensure complete coverage.

Where you start stitching the design is usually a matter of personal preference, but it is often easiest to stitch the outline first. Thread your needle (using a needle threader, if required), and bring the needle up through the fabric for the first stitch. Leave a short length of thread (about 3" (7.5 cm)) behind the fabric and secure this in place with the first few stitches. Once you have used up the thread, take the end back through to the reverse of the fabric and secure it in place by running it through the back of the last stitches. Later threads can be secured by running through the backs of earlier stitches. Do not use knots as they will make the work look uneven.

If you make a mistake, unpick the stitches very carefully. It is tempting simply to cut the incorrect threads, but be warned that it is very easy to also cut the fabric by mistake. It is usually better to unpick the stitches in the reverse direction to the order in which they were sewn – i.e. unpick the last stitch first. Remember you must unpick all the stitches completed with that strand of thread or secure the end firmly, otherwise the remaining stitches will work loose.

Stitches

The stitches here only cover a fraction of what is available. As I said earlier, any combination of threads is possible. These stitches will give you a good base from which to work: they are all fairly simple, can be worked on any fabric with any thread and, when combined, give limitless possibilities of pattern and design. They have been grouped roughly according to the type of stitch, but are not in any order of difficulty as most are simple once you have mastered the technique. Look through the stitches and when you find one you like practise it on a small piece of fabric. Some may look fiddly, but you will soon find how easy and effective they really are.

Flat stitches

Running stitch
This is the most basic stitch, but can be very effective. Be careful that all the stitches and gaps are of equal length.

■ Running stitch

An interesting variation can be to work a thread of a different colour in between the stitches. Be very careful not to pull the thread too tight.

■ Threaded running stitch.

Back stitch

This is also known as *point de sable* stitch, and is very useful for outlines as it produces a solid line of a single colour. In each stitch the needle is carried back before the next stitch is made.

Back stitch can also be threaded in a similar way to running stitch.

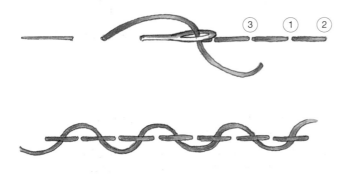

■ Back stitch. Bring the needle up at 1 and down through 2, completing the first stitch. Then bring the needle up through at 3 and carry it back down again at 1 to complete the second stitch. Be careful all the stitches are even. The drawing also shows threaded back stitch.

Stem stitch

This is also known as *crewel stitch*, and produces a slightly thicker line. It is known as stem stitch as it is particularly useful for stitching the stems of flowers.

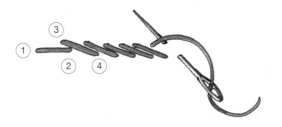

■ Stem stitch. Bring the needle up through the fabric at 1 and down again through 2 to complete the first stitch. Then bring the needle up at 3, midway between 1 and 2. Carry that stitch forward to 4 to complete the second stitch. Be careful that you always come up on the same side of the previous stitch.

Split stitch

This is another stitch which is useful for outlines. It is worked in exactly the same way as stem stitch except that the needle is brought up through the threads of the previous stitch rather than to one side of them.

■ Split stitch.

Satin stitch

Satin stitch is one of the most important embroidery stitches and is used for filling in areas. It consists of stitches placed side by side to completely cover the surface of the fabric. It appears simple, but it takes some practice to get the coverage absolutely even. It is very useful for infilling small areas, but over large areas the stitches can work loose. For anything over $\frac{3}{4}$" (2 cm) it would be better to divide the area with a row of back stitch or use a different method.

The direction in which these stitches lie is very important. Look carefully at the design before you begin stitching as the direction you choose will influence the way the light reflects off the area and the look of the filled space.

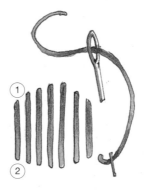

■ Satin and brick satin stitch. Bring the needle up through at the bottom of the area at 1 and carry it down through at the top at 2. The next stitch must lie exactly beside the previous one and parallel to it. It is important that the stitches do not overlap and that they lie flat on the fabric.

Brick satin stitch

Straight stitch

This is a single satin stitch which can be any length and lie in any direction.

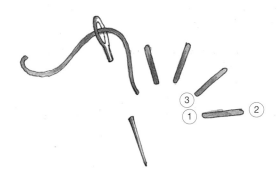

A variation of satin stitch is *brick satin stitch*, which can be used for filling large areas. Work four stitches as shown in the drawing and then work the next four slightly less than half the length. Continue this to the end of the area. The next row should be worked in the long stitches, each starting at the end of the stitch in the previous row.

■ Working straight stitch. Bring the needle up at 1 and down through at 2. Then carry across the back to begin the next stitch at 3. Try to avoid carrying the thread too far across the back of the fabric.

Long and short stitch

This is a very useful stitch for infilling large areas and for gradually blending colours across an area. It is worked in a similar way to brick satin stitch (above), but each individual stitch is staggered. The first row of stitches consists of long and short stitches as shown in the drawing. It is important that the outer line of the stitches is kept even. Complete the second row with long stitches, each one passing through the tip of the previous stitch. The final row will consist of long and short stitches to complete the infilling.

This stitch is very useful for flowers and animals where irregular variations of colour give a more lifelike appearance.

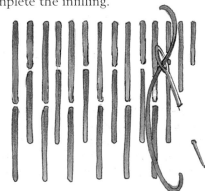

■ Long and short stitch.

Seeding

Seeding consists of very small, randomly placed running stitches and is useful for infilling areas. Be careful to ensure that the stitches are completely random – they should all face different directions and the spaces in between should be reasonably even. If you wish to create a more solid appearance, place two stitches next to each other, as shown in the figure.

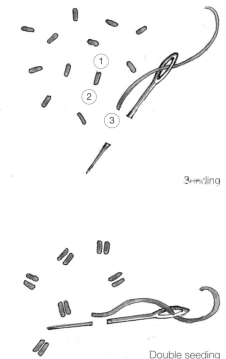

Seeding

■ Seeding. Bring the needle up at 1 and down through 2. Bring it up at 3 for the next stitch. Also double seeding.

Double seeding

Looped stitches

These stitches consist of a loop of thread which is held in place with another stitch. Chain stitch and blanket stitch are the most widely used.

Chain stitch

This can be used as a single outline, a solid infilling stitch or as individual loops. At first it may seem very fiddly, but once you have practised a few stitches you will see it is actually very easy. When you get to the last stitch, secure it in place with a single running stitch.

For infilling, simply work rows of chain stitch next to each other.

detail

■ Chain stitch. Bring the needle up through the fabric at 1 and then insert the needle back down through the same hole, carrying the thread under the point of the needle. Hold the loop down with your left thumb and bring the needle back up through the fabric at 2 where the next stitch will begin. Pull the thread so it lies flat, but be careful not to pull it so tight that the loop disappears. Lazy daisy stitch, a variant of chain stitch, is useful for making small flower petals.

A variation is *lazy daisy* or *detached chain stitch*. Each stitch is worked individually and fixed in place with a small stitch as in the last stitch of a row. As shown in the drawing, form a loop in the usual way and then bring the needle up at 2 at the end of the loop. Pass it back down through 3 to hold the loop in place and then bring it up through the fabric at 4 to begin the next stitch. This is particularly useful for making simple flower petals – hence its name!

Blanket stitch

This is also known as *buttonhole stitch* and is frequently used to protect fabric at the edges of blankets or round buttonholes.

It is important that the base stitches and uprights are all kept as even as possible. A great many variations can be achieved by varying the length of the stitches and the angle at which they are aligned.

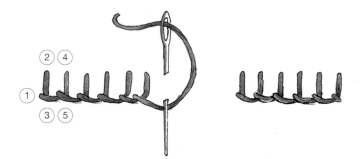

■ Working blanket stitch. Bring the needle up through the fabric at 1. Push it down through 2 and out again at 3, keeping the thread looped under the point of the needle, as shown in the drawing. Continue the next stitch by pushing the needle down through 4 and up again at 5. Secure the last stitch with a small running stitch as shown.

Lazy daisy or detached chain stitich

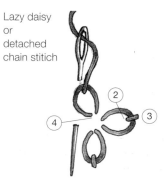

Fly stitch

Also known as open loop or Y stitch, this can be worked in rows, groups or individually.

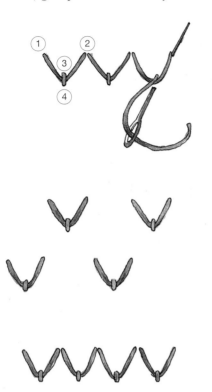

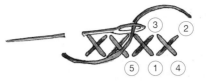

■ Cross stitch. Bring the needle up at 1 and down through 2 to form the first stitch. Then bring it up at 3 and down again through 4, completing the first cross. Bring the needle up again at 5 to start the next cross.

Ermine stitch

This is one of the many variations of cross stitch and consists of a straight stitch underneath an elongated cross stitch. It was frequently used in Spanish black work and its name originates from the ermine effect when it is worked in black thread on a white background.

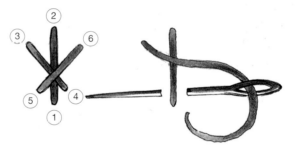

■ Fly stitches can be worked individually, or placed in groups and rows to give different effects. Bring the needle up through the fabric at the top of the stitch at 1. Pass it down through the other arm of the stitch at 2. Make sure the two arms are level. Come up at 3 and secure the base of the arms with a small running stitch to 4.

Crossed stitches

These are one of the oldest types of stitches, as described in the chapter on cross stitch. They consist of two straight stitches which cross each other – usually at right angles. The stitch lengths can be varied, creating endless possibilities.

Always ensure that the lengths of the stitches are equal (unless the pattern dictates otherwise) and that the top stitches all face the same way.

■ Ermine stitch is one of the many possible variations of cross stitch. Bring the needle up at 1 and back down at 2 to form the upright straight stitch. Then follow 3 to 6 to form the cross on top. Each stitch of the cross should be about two-thirds of the length of the upright stitch.

Couching

This method was originally used to secure threads which were too brittle or valuable to pass through the fabric. It is particularly useful for working with gold or other metal threads.

Bring the thread which is to be stitched over up through to the right side of the fabric, having secured it on the reverse. Using another needle, bring the securing thread up and work small stitches over the other thread to hold it in place.

Couching can be used instead of satin stitch to completely cover large areas, or can be varied to form trellis work. This trellis work is frequently called *battlemented couching* or *Jacobean couching* as it was popular in seventeenth-century English embroideries. As shown in the drawing, the laid or under stitches are worked to form a trellis pattern. These lines are then held in place with small stitches, which cover the two threads at each intersection. A great many variations are possible in the number of threads used, the type of securing stitch and even stitches within the squares of the trellis. Examples are shown in the drawing.

French knot

The French knot is a raised stitch which looks like a small bead. Whole embroidery patterns can be created with it but usually it is used to create a speckled effect, for the centres of flowers or for the eyes of animals and birds.

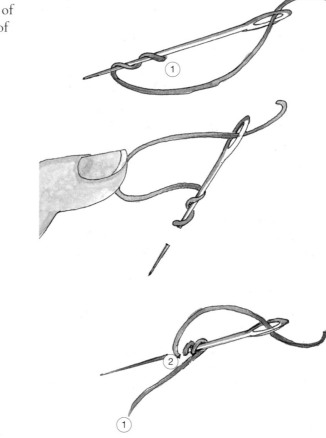

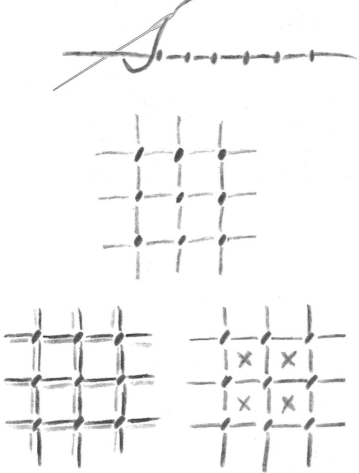

■ Some of the many variations possible with couching.

■ French knots. Bring the needle up at 1 and then twist the thread twice round the needle. Insert the needle back down near to 1 and gently pull the thread through to the back of the canvas. Hold the thread steady with your left hand so the knot forms as near to the fabric as possible. A variation is to create a stem for the knot to sit on: this is useful for rows of small flowers. Work as before, but instead of inserting the needle back through the fabric, carry it across to 2 and then pull it through.

Infilling

A variety of stitches are useful for filling in areas of fabric. Many are combinations of two or more stitches and you will soon see that the variations possible are endless.

Brick and cross

This consists of squares of satin stitch with crosses between.

Work the squares of satin stitch first and then stitch the crosses in between as shown in the figure. Finally secure the centre of each cross with a small upright stitch.

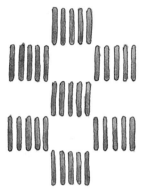

Variants on brick and cross stitch

Weaving stitch

This is a trellis stitch which is held in place by a woven thread which works across the intersections. Be very careful not to pull the trellis threads too tight because the fabric will pucker.

Weaving stitch

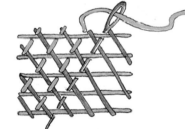

Work the horizontal threads first, as shown in the drawing. Next, stitch the second row of diagonal threads. Finally take the third colour and weave it between the intersections of the first two colours. This third thread should pass under the first line of threads and over the second line.

Cloud stitch

This is also called *Mexican stitch*, and was very popular in seventeenth-century Jacobean embroidery.

First work the outline pattern of small vertical stitches as shown in the drawing. The stitches should be just large enough to allow two threads to pass through them, otherwise they will dominate the pattern. Then thread the second colour through these stitches as shown to form a trellis.

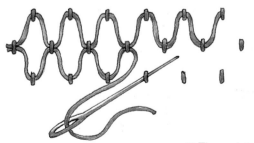

Cloud stitch

 The variety of patterns you can make with infilling stitches is almost limitless.

Burden stitch

Burden stitch is a type of couching that can be used to create a woven effect if woollen threads are used. The base lines are worked as shown in the drawing. Smaller vertical stitches are then worked from alternate lines, passing over the central line. Work each line in turn.

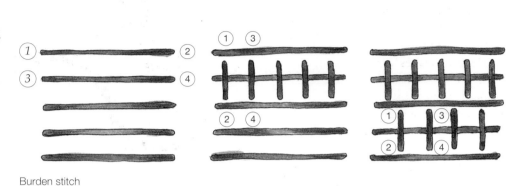

Burden stitch

Miscellaneous stitches

These stitches do not fit into any particular category but are nevertheless useful. They are also good examples of how easily stitches can be combined.

Chevron stitch

This consists of diagonal stitches between two parallel lines of stitches and is useful for borders.

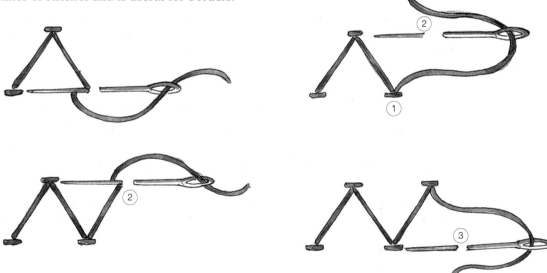

■ Chevron stitch is particularly useful for borders. Begin on the bottom row and stitch a back stitch as shown in the drawing. Bring the thread up in the centre of the stitch at 1 and make a diagonal stitch at 2. Work another back stitch parallel to the first with 2 as the centre of the stitch. Bring the needle up again at 2 and carry to 3 to form the next diagonal line. Carry on in this way to form a continuous line. Note that the back stitches should be considerably smaller than the diagonals.

Fern stitch

This is a fine, delicate stitch which is particularly useful for marking on leaves. It is made up of three equal straight stitches which radiate from a single point on a line.

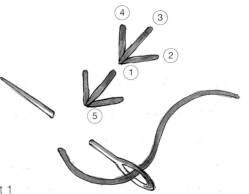

■ Preparing fern stitch. Bring the needle up at 1 and down at 2 to form the first stitch. Carry the thread across to come out at 3 and form the central stitch or stem by passing the thread back down through 1. Bring the needle up at 4 and back down again through 1 to complete the stitch. Bring the thread up at 5 to start the next stitch.

Sheaf stitch

This is also called *faggot stitch* as it resembles the bundles into which corn or kindling sticks used to be bound. It consists of three vertical satin stitches which are bound together.

■ Sheaf stitch. Form three satin stitches and then bring the thread up through the fabric to one side of the stitches in the centre at 1. Pass the needle round the three vertical threads without piercing the fabric. Pass the fabric over the three threads again and back down through the fabric at 2.

Types of embroidery

You will have realised by now that the term 'embroidery' covers a wide range of stitches and techniques. Some of these stitches can be combined to form particular kinds of embroidery. Of these the most well known are described briefly below, though instructions on how to work them are not given. I hope that the descriptions will give you an idea of what is involved in these techniques and perhaps help you to recognise them as you explore the huge variety of work that embroidery has to offer.

Assisi

Assisi work is a type of cross stitch (see next chapter) usually worked around the border of a piece in a single colour. The designs are outlined but left blank while the background is infilled with cross stitch. It is named after the town of Assisi in Italy but may have originated from copies of pieces of dark wood inlaid with patterns of Egyptian ivory and pearls.

Black work

This is also known as *Holbein work* or *Spanish work* and was most popular in sixteenth-century Europe. It is traditionally worked in black silk on white linen and consists of outlined shapes filled with repetitive patterns. It became very popular because the printed designs were easy to copy from books.

Crewel work

This term was originally used to describe Jacobean work which consisted of formal scrolling patterns with birds, animals and Tree of Life designs. It is now used to describe most types of embroidery worked in wool rather than silk or cotton.

Open work

A large group of techniques all involve removing part of the base fabric or creating holes in it. In *drawn fabric* (also called pulled fabric, pulled work, punch work, *punto a giorno* or *a jour* embroidery) the threads are pulled together to create holes. In *drawn thread* (*punto tagliato*) some of the warp and weft threads are actually removed. In fine work it is easy to confuse this with drawn fabric. *Hardanger embroidery* originated in Norway; blocks of satin stitches called klosters are worked round squares of fabric, which are then cut away. The final type of open work is *cut work*. This is worked on closely woven fabric and the outline of the design is stitched in running stitch. Blanket stitch is then worked over these lines and the inner area cut away to reveal the pattern.

Stump work

This was most popular in seventeenth-century Britain and consisted of heavily worked panels which were frequently made into boxes. Hanks of wool or hair were used to create the stumps, which were then stitched over until the desired shape was achieved. Silk, beads, jewels and shiny metals were used to decorate the piece, which was usually a picture with figures and animals.

White work

Any white stitching on a white or unbleached background can be referred to as white work, but one of the most famous types came from the Mountmellick workshop in Ireland. Flowers were worked in heavy thread on fine satin, creating interesting textures. In the nineteenth century work declined in Ireland and many people were saved from starvation by exporting white work.

Project 1 · Dragon tray

This dragon is based on the Chinese folk tale of the ice dragon who breathed snow and ice rather than fire.

Equipment needed

- Tray (available from needlecraft shops)
- 28# cotton or linen mix 14" × 11" (35 × 28 cm) (check tray size)
- Size 24 tapestry needle or size 5 crewel needle
- DMC stranded cotton using three strands:

Ice Blue	3753	two skeins
Navy	336	half skein
Purple	327	one skein
Turquoise	806	half skein
Yellow	725	two strands
Red	816	one strand
Turquoise	930	one skein
	931	half skein
	932	half skein
	3752	half skein
Grey	317	one strand

■ Right: The completed dragon tray.

■ Template for the
Dragon design.

Working the design

Prepare the fabric as described earlier in the chapter.
Transfer the design from the template onto the fabric.
I cut out a template and drew round it, but you could
use dressmaker's carbon or pounce if you prefer.
Stitch the outline of the body first and then infill,
following the instructions on the chart.

■ Pattern for the
Dragon design.

Embroidery dragon stitches

- **Spines**   outlined in stem stitch, infilled with satin.
- **Body**   upper outline in blanket stitch, lower outline in two rows of back stitch, staggered. Infilled with lengths of chain stitch, anything from one to eleven stitches long.
- **Tail**   navy outline and turquoise inner line in stem stitch. Infilled with satin stitch.

- **Feet**   Legs and feet infilling in chain stitch. Claws in two stitches of stem stitch.
- **Face**   All outlines in stem stitch, mouth in back stitch, nostrils in single chain stitch, eyes in French knots edged with yellow back stitch. Eyebrows in purple satin stitch worked in two groups of stitches.

The character of the dragon could be changed by using different colours and fabric backings. Red and gold would give the finished piece a fiery look, whereas greens and turquoises are more subtle.

Finishing

When you have finished, press the fabric with a warm iron under a damp cloth and assemble the tray following the manufacturer's instructions.

If you wanted, this dragon could be framed in a picture or used to cover a decorative box.

Project 2 ·
Crewel chess board

Crewel wool on a cotton–linen mix has been used to create this chess board. The broad, flat frame provides an ideal place for chess pieces. In a similar way to the square picture project in the chapter on ornamental needlepoint, this could be used as a type of sampler and you could easily substitute any stitches you particularly like.

Equipment

- 28# cotton–linen mix 14" (35 cm) square
- 10 crewel needle
- Appleton crewel wool using one strand (one skein each):
- Turquoise 566

■ {	Dark Red	948
	Red	946
	Pink	944
■ {	Dark Green	835
	Mid Green	833
	Light Green	831
■ {	Dark Purple	105
	Mid Purple	103
	Light Purple	102
■ {	Dark Blue	852
	Mid Blue	565
	Light Blue	563

Preparing

Prepare the fabric as described earlier in the chapter and divide the centre into 64 squares, each one measuring just under 1" (2.5 cm). You can either count 27 stitches per square or draw it out with a ruler and specialist pen. Then fill in the alternate squares, which will form the black squares of the chess board. Either follow the chart on page 29 or choose your own stitches. Finally stitch large diagonal stitches as the border.

■ This chess board would look equally good framed as a sampler.

Stitching

A Battlemented couching: Make three horizontal and vertical lines. Work in all three shades, using the darkest first. Also use the darkest for the small fixing stitches.

B Blanket stitch: Work five rows of blanket stitch across the square.

C Brick stitch: Work blocks of five satin stitches, each covering five threads of the fabric.

D Brick and cross stitch: Work as above, then position crosses in between in a contrasting shade and fix in the centre with a small upright stitch.

E Brick satin stitch: Begin at the base of the square and work along in groups of five stitches, with the longer stitches covering six threads and the shorter covering three. Use the darkest shade first, then the middle, then the palest and then the middle shade again.

F Burden stitch: Work six horizontal rows in the darkest shade. Hold in place with vertical stitches in the middle shade.

G Chain filling: Work from the outside inwards, completing two rows of chain stitch in each colour, starting with the darkest shade. Also complete the centre in the darkest shade.

H Cloud: Work seven rows of small upright stitches in the palest shade. Thread the middle shade through these stitches.

I Couched trellis: Work three horizontal and vertical rows in the middle shade. Hold in place with small diagonal stitches in the palest shade.

J Couched trellis diagonal: Work as above, but use the darker shade to lay nine diagonal lines each way across the square.

K Ermine: Place five ermine stitches centrally in the square.

L Fern stitch: Work a line of curved fern stitch diagonally across the square.

	G	M		C		F
O		A		I		E
	J		H		K	G
E		N		D		L
	H		B		F	N
L		E		P		D
	K		G		L	E
D		H		C		O

■ Chart for the chess board project.

M Fly stitch: Place seven fly stitches centrally in the square.

N French knot: Place five groups of french knots centrally in the square. Each group should consist of three french knots on stems radiating out from a central point.

O Sheaf: Place five sheaf stitches in two horizontal rows. Use a contrasting colour for the central horizontal stitches.

P Weaving stitch: Weave across the square using all three shades.

Complete the pattern with two rows of large angled back stitches round the edge in dark red and purple.

Finishing

When you have finished, press the piece under a damp cloth with a warm iron. Put into a frame with a broad, flat edge. Any framer can do this for you.

Project 3 ·
Elizabethan flowers

This design of flowers is very similar to those which were popular in Elizabethan England – in the sixteenth and early seventeenth century. The thick matte cotton stands out well against the linen.

Equipment needed

Blue bag

- 28# linen 24" × 15" (60 × 38 cm)
- 24 tapestry needle or 5 crewel needle
- 48" (120 cm) of braid
- Matte/soft embroidery thread (one skein each). Anchor using three strands:
- Pale Green   213 ·
- Mid Green   215
- Bright Green   923
- Gold   302
- Yellow   300
- Pale Pink   839
- Dark Pink   690
- Turquoise   168
- Brown   310

Green bag

- 28# linen 18" (45 cm) square
- 24 tapestry needle or 5 crewel needle
- 30" (75 cm) of braid
- Matte/soft embroidery thread (one skein each). Anchor using three strands:
- Pale Green   213
- Mid Green   215
- Navy   127
- Gold   302
- Yellow   300
- Pale Pink   839
- Dark Pink   690
- Pale Blue   161
- Brown   310

If you wish to make both large and small bags, one skein of each colour should be enough.

■ Above: blue and green drawstring bags.

■ Right: close-up of the motif for tablecloth and napkins.

Tablecloth

- Tablecloth (cotton or linen) 72" × 52" (180 × 130 cm)
- Four napkins (cotton or linen)
- Crewel needle 5
- DMC stranded cotton using three strands:

Dark Blue	791	two skeins
Pale Blue	799	two and a half skeins
Beige	841	one skein
Cream	842	one skein

see photograph above

Working the designs

Prepare the fabric as described earlier in the chapter. Transfer the design onto the fabric using the template. Either cut a template and draw round it or transfer the design using dressmaker's carbon or pounce. Work the design following the stitches given.

Flowers: Work the outlines in back stitch. The yellow centre is satin stitch. Six straight stitches complete the flower. For variations mix the red and pink – for example, two strands of red and one strand of pink.

Stem: Couching, held in place with small brown stitches.

■ Template for the Elizabethan flowers bag.

■ Chart for the Elizabethan flowers.

Pineapples: The base is worked in pale and mid green, using long and short stitch. The outline of the fruit is worked in gold using back stitch and the centre consists of three straight stitches and seeding in yellow. The leaves are bright green and can be worked in stem stitch, or split stitch for variation. The centres of the leaves have two joined chain stitches and two single chain stitches on either side, worked in pale blue.

Small leaves: These are worked in stem stitch, again using a mixture of pale and mid green.

The top of the bag is decorated with a line of threaded running stitch using gold and yellow.

When you have finished, press the fabric with a warm iron under a damp cloth and make up the bag following the instructions on page 106.

For the tablecloth I used stranded cotton rather than matte cotton as it lies flatter. Also I could not find the colours I wanted in matte cotton and stranded cottons come in a wider range. All this is personal preference: anything could easily be altered. The amounts given above include four corner panels and twenty flowers randomly placed in the centre of the cloth. Work the pattern in two shades of blue using similar stitches to the drawstring bags. One skein each of the beige and cream is ample for four napkins. Enlarge the template for the napkins (figure opposite) until it is 1" (2.5 cm) from the edge of the napkin. Transfer the wavy line onto the napkin and add a single flower in one corner. If you are using different colours for the cloth and napkins, ensure that the embroidery thread on the cloth matches the napkins and vice versa.

When stitching this pattern, remember that in reality all flowers vary. Don't worry if all the leaves are not exactly symmetrical and intermix the shades to give subtle variations to each plant.

■ The Elizabethan flowers motif works very well on this tablecloth.

■ Templates for
the tablecloth
and napkins.

3

Cross stitch

Cross stitch is one of the oldest embroidery stitches. Archaeological evidence shows us that embroidery frames, which had been used to support pieces of cross stitch, were often put in the tombs of aristocratic Egyptian ladies. Its enduring popularity is probably due to the fact that it is one of the easiest and most adaptable stitches.

The traditional embroidery of many countries like Turkey and the Scandinavian countries uses cross stitch as the main stitch. It has been adapted in countries such as Yemen and Algeria to produce herringbone. In folk art cross stitch is traditionally considered to bring good luck and keep evil away and it is used commonly for special articles and garments.

Pattern books for cross stitch were common in Europe in the early sixteenth century. Designs were taken from these and sold on in the form of woodcuts and, later, engravings. It was not until the eighteenth century, with the advent of magazines, that patterns and instructions became widely available.

The history of samplers deserves a separate mention. The oldest example of a sampler goes back to AD 850 in Chinese Turkestan and contains 28 different patterns. Early samplers were produced to demonstrate skill in different forms of stitches and to act as a useful reference of stitches to be handed down through the generations. From the eighth century onwards in Europe, girls of the nobility were taught to sew in convent schools and right up till the mid-nineteenth century needlework was felt to be a suitable occupation for the womenfolk of the upper classes, who could not work and therefore had plenty of time on their hands. In the eighteenth and nineteenth centuries utilitarian samplers developed. They were usually worked in one colour with as much variation of pattern as possible and were produced to demonstrate to prospective employers the skill of the needlewoman. At that time any woman employed in domestic service was expected to be proficient with a needle and thread.

The style and subject matter of samplers varied over the years. In the eighteenth century designs were heavily influenced by imported Indian cottons and the patterns became more flowery and ornate. Religious motifs were always a popular subject. Of course cross stitch was not the only stitch to be worked on samplers – other stitches like back stitch, satin stitch and Florentine stitch were popular – but cross stitch nearly always predominated and for this reason it is frequently called sampler stitch.

In the twentieth century, social change and the arrival of the sewing machine led to a decline in the working of the traditional sampler, but cross stitch remains a popular form of needlework and is thriving in new and exciting ways throughout the world.

Equipment

As with embroidery, a wide range of fabrics can be used for cross stitch. Some are especially designed for it, like Aida and Binca, but most firm fabrics can be used with the aid of waste canvas, as described in Chapter 1. Both projects in this chapter are worked on 14# Aida. This is a basketweave fabric designed for cross stitch and the holes are easy to see without having to use waste canvas. Needlecraft shops also sell a range of household items such as towels and bedspreads with borders of Aida to enable you to decorate them with cross stitch. Other fabrics you may have come across include Jobelan, which is a mixture of cotton and modal woven in single threads similar to linen. It is easy to wash and comes in over 40 different colours. Linda looks like linen and is similar to stitch on but is made of cotton and synthetics, which makes it useful for items that need frequent washing, like tablecloths or children's items. Paper canvas can also be used as a base for cross stitch designs. It was widely used during Victorian times in England, when it was referred to as punched paper and used for bookmarks, cards, boxes and needlecases. It is easy to work with as long as you take the following precautions: do not fold the paper unless it is to be a permanent part of the design, make sure you use it the right way up (the top side is smoother) and always remember that paper is not as tough as fabric so treat it gently.

As with other types of embroidery, almost any thread can be used for cross stitch as long as it is compatible with the base fabric. Stranded cotton is the most commonly used as the individual strands are easy to divide and mix and therefore can be adapted to suit most fabric weights. Before you start, all the threads should be cut to a manageable length – about 30" (75 cm).

If you are dealing with a lot of colours, you may find it easier to manage them if you make a card organiser such as the one shown below. These can be bought from specialist shops, but it is easy to make your own. Take a firm piece of card and punch holes down either side. Label each hole with the manufacturer's code number and then loop the cut lengths of thread through and secure them.

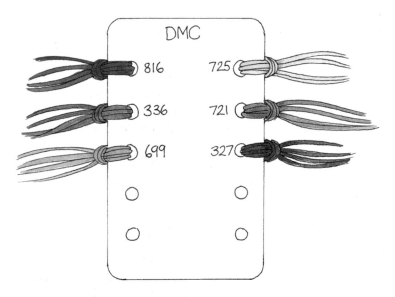

■ Using a simple thread organiser, which you can create by punching holes in a piece of card, will help you to work.

The thickness of thread you use will depend both on the ground fabric and the effect you want to achieve. A general rule is that thick threads will create a bolder design – for example, four strands of stranded cotton on 14# would create a solid pattern whereas two strands would produce a finer, more delicate effect. If in doubt, test the strands on a piece of spare fabric. It is usually better to stick to the same number of strands throughout a piece because the stitches may look uneven otherwise.

The needle you use will vary according to the fabric you have chosen. Crewel needles will be useful for even-weave fabrics, whereas blunt-ended tapestry needles are more suitable for fabrics like Aida where the holes are already marked. If you are not sure which to use, test the needles out by pushing them through the fabric; they should slide through easily without enlarging the hole in the fabric. In many cases the choice will be up to you – some people only use crewel needles while others are convinced that tapestry needles are far better.

Whether or not you use a frame is entirely a matter of personal choice. If you stick to the method of stitching described in this chapter your fabric should not distort at all, but for large projects on even-weave fabrics many people find a frame easier to manage.

Close attention is essential for cross stitch. It is perfectly possible to fill in backgrounds of needlepoint while watching television, but this is not possible with cross stitch. Here each stitch must be evenly and correctly placed and for this you also need good light. Daylight is obviously ideal, but ordinary electric light is perfectly satisfactory. Daylight bulbs are available from specialist suppliers and are very useful because many people's free (and therefore stitching) time occurs in the evening. Specialist magnifying anglepoise lamps are also available and can be useful if you are doing a lot of fine work. If stitching on dark colours (e.g. the black fabric of the ice dragon) it is useful to have a pale background underneath the fabric. If you spread white paper or a pale cloth on the table at which you are working, this will show through the dark fabric and make the holes much easier to see.

Most cross stitch is worked off a chart similar to that used in needlepoint, each square on the chart representing one stitch on the fabric. The size of the finished design will depend on the fabric you are using – a design worked on 28# linen will be half the size of the same design worked on 14# Aida. To calculate the design size, count the number of stitches on the chart horizontally and vertically and then divide these numbers by the gauge of the canvas. This will give you the size in inches of the finished design. For example, a line of 60 stitches would be just over 2" (5 cm) long if worked on 28# and nearly 4½" (12 cm) long if worked on 14#.

Once you get used to the discipline of counting, charts are very easy to use because you always know exactly where you are. Where you start is a matter of choice. The centre is often the easiest point to work out from, but depending on the design it may be easiest to stitch the outlines first.

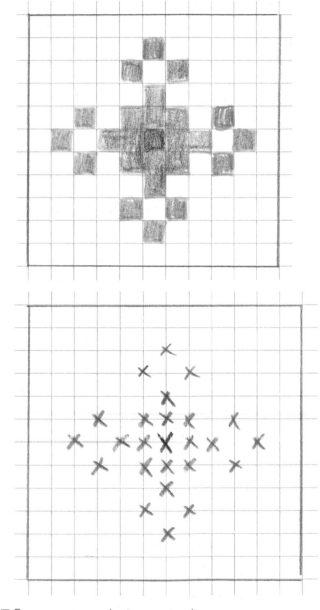

■ One square on a chart corresponds to one stitch on the fabric.

Starting

Before starting make sure you have enough fabric for the project you want to complete. This is particularly important if you are stitching directly onto the fabric that will form the finished object – such as a tablecloth. With pieces where the stitched fabric will be added to the finished piece, like a panel on a bag, it is only important that you have enough fabric to contain your design. Ideally allow a 2" (5 cm) border all round.

The edges of the fabric need to be secured or they will fray. You can either fold them over and hem round the piece or stitch protective binding tape round it. If using tape, place it over the edge of the fabric so half is above and half below. Then tack round, making sure that both sides of tape are attached to the fabric. Fold the tape over at the corners to ensure complete coverage.

When casting on and off *never* use knots as this will make the work uneven. For the first stitch keep about $1\frac{1}{2}$" (4 cm) of thread beneath the fabric and secure it in place with the first line of stitches. Once you have stitched the first length of thread, later pieces can be secured by threading them through the back of already completed stitches. As you get to the end of each piece of thread, pull it through to the back of the fabric and run it through the back of adjacent stitches. This will secure it properly and ensure that the stitches do not work loose.

Stitches

There are two different ways to work cross stitch, but in both cases the important rule to remember is that all the top stitches must lie facing the same direction. If you are working without a frame, it is also important to remember that all the threads at the back of the fabric should travel horizontally or vertically as this will prevent the fabric from distorting.

The first method involves stitching all the lower halves of the crosses and then working back completing the top stitches, as shown in the drawing.

With the second method each stitch is completed individually. This is an easier method to use if much counting or changing colour is involved.

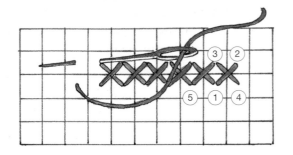

■ Cross stitch method 2. Bring the needle up through the fabric at 1 and travel over one diagonal intersection to 2. Bring the needle up at 3 and complete the stitch by travelling back across the same intersection to 4. Then pass the needle under two threads of canvas to start the next stitch at 5. Note that the needle always travels parallel to the canvas at the back and not diagonally. This is particularly important when changing direction. Make sure that all your top stitches are facing the same way.

With either method you need to be very careful, when stitching a diagonal line or changing direction, to ensure all the stitches are correct. This may sound obvious, but it is surprisingly easy to go wrong. At the end of each stitch you need to position the needle carefully so that when you move on, the thread on the reverse of the fabric is still travelling vertically or horizontally. It doesn't matter if it goes diagonally on the reverse occasionally but the more often this happens the more likely the fabric is to distort and need stretching at the end.

■ Cross stitch method 1. Bring the needle up at 1 and down through the fabric diagonally across one intersection of fabric at 2. Then bring the needle up at 3, immediately below 2. Continue in this way, ensuring that all the diagonal lines at the front face the same way and that all the threads travel across the back of the fabric either vertically or horizontally. When you have reached the end of the row, travel back as shown to complete the crosses.

At some point you are bound to make a mistake which needs to be unpicked. It may seem easiest simply to cut the incorrect threads, but be warned – it is also very easy to cut the fabric by mistake. It is much safer to unpick the stitches in the reverse direction to the order in which they were sewn – i.e. unpick the last stitch first. Remember you must unpick all the stitches completed with that strand of thread, or secure the end firmly, otherwise the remaining stitches will work loose.

Project 1 · Dragon picture

This piece is based on the Chinese Ice Dragon Project which was featured in Chapter 2. This shows how different a design can look if stitched in a different technique. The illustration on page 8 shows a further variation, where the same pattern is worked with wool on canvas.

Equipment needed

- Picture frame 6" × 8" (15 × 20 cm)
- 14# black Aida 10" × 12" (25 × 30 cm)
- Tapestry needle size 22
- DMC stranded cotton using three strands.

Red	816	one strand
Yellow	725	half skein
Orange	721	one strand
White	3072	half skein
Pale Blue	3753	one and a half skeins
Turquoise	924	half skein
Pale Turquoise	926	one and a half skeins
Grey	317	half skein
Dark Purple	550	half skein
Pale Purple	327	half skein
Blue	336	half skein

Working the design

Prepare the fabric as described earlier. Fold the fabric in quarters to find the centre.

You will probably find it easiest to stitch the outline of the body first. It is very important at this stage that you position all the stitches correctly as everything else will depend on this outline. This will be fiddly and time-consuming but once completed everything else falls into place easily.

When you have finished, press the fabric with a warm iron under a damp cloth and insert into the picture frame. If you are framing it yourself, tape any excess fabric firmly down with masking tape to hold the picture in place.

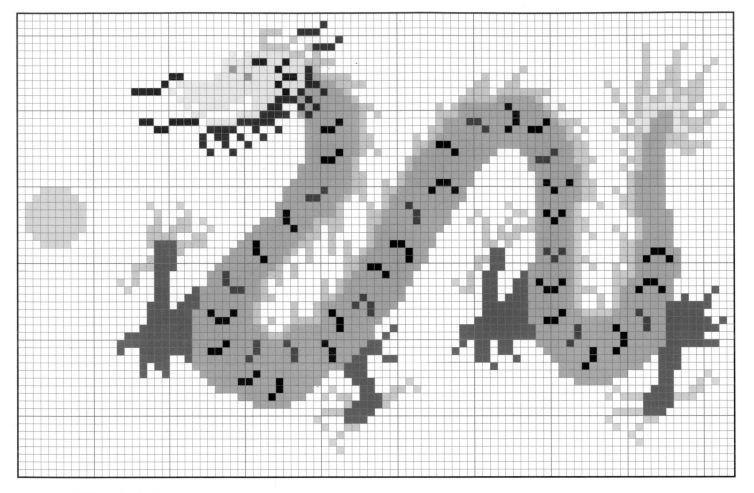

■ Chart for the Ice
Dragon design.

If you wish, this chart could also be used with wool on
canvas to create a dragon similar to the one on page 8.
The finished size would of course depend on the gauge
of canvas you used.

The finished picture complete with frame can be seen
in the photograph opposite. Notice how the dragon
worked in cross stitch looks very different from the
same design in embroidery (page 25).

■ Right: The completed
dragon picture.

Project 2 ·
Mexican book cover

This bright and colourful book cover is based on
beadwork designs. The Mexicans use these in
jewellery or as adornments for clothes. The sizes
given below will cover an average paperback, but if
you have a particular book in mind always check its
dimensions as the thickness of the book will alter the
overall size.

Equipment needed

■ 14# red Aida 11" × 14" (28 × 35 cm)
■ Lining fabric (thin cotton) two pieces 10" × 6"
   (23 × 15 cm)
■ DMC stranded cotton using three strands:

■	Dark Blue	336	one skein
■	Turquoise	806	one skein
■	Yellow	725	one skein
■	Green	699	one skein
■	White	712	one skein
■	Orange	722	half skein

■ The completed
book cover.

Working the design

Prepare the fabric as described earlier. Fold in half lengthwise and mark the central fold (a couple of tacking stitches is enough). This is the line which will go along the centre of the spine of the book.

Stitch the central blue pattern first. Then measure the fabric carefully against the book you are going to cover, placing the blue pattern exactly along the spine of the book. Mark the four corners of the book on each half of the fabric with tacking stitches and then find the centre of each half by folding the fabric as before.

centre line ⟶

■ Chart for the Mexican book cover project.

How you complete the stitches is a matter of personal preference: you can either work outwards from the centre or complete the yellow outlines first. When you have completed the blue and yellow patterns, remove the binding tape and fold the fabric over just outside the eight marks you made earlier. The fabric should now be slightly larger than the book. If necessary tack to ensure a neat edge. Then work the two rows of alternate green stitches through both layers of fabric.

Finally press under a damp cloth using a warm iron and make up following the instructions on page 105.

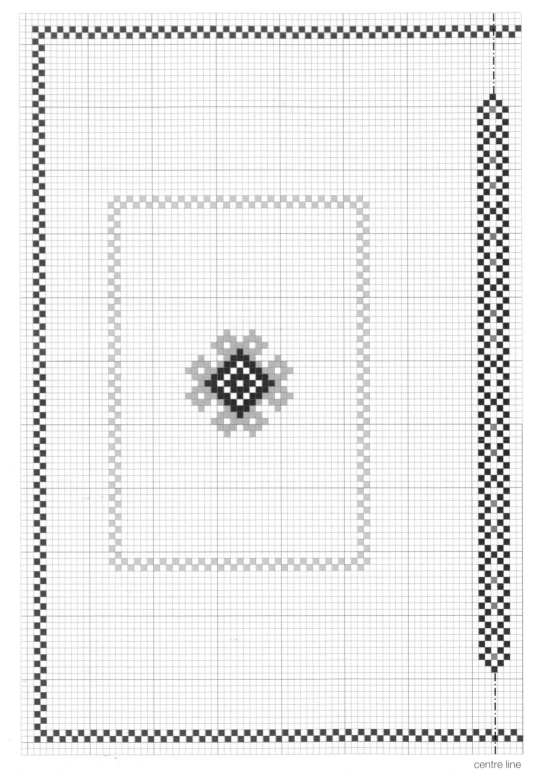

■ Chart for the Mexican Book Cover project.

centre line

4

Needlepoint

Needlepoint is the strongest and most hardwearing of all types of needlecraft. Throughout the ages it has been used for chair covers, cushions and wall hangings. The stitches completely cover the ground and this strengthens as well as decorates it.

Needlepoint tapestries were made by the Egyptians and Phrygians and the Romans called it *opus pulvinarium* (cushion work) and used it to decorate the cushions on which they lounged.

Since medieval times needlepoint has been closely associated with the Christian Church and even today is used for hangings, kneelers, altar fronts and vestments.

In Tudor times in England, tapestries were frequently copied in needlepoint, and during the sixteenth century it became increasingly popular throughout Europe. With the opening up of the trade routes, carpets and embroideries were imported from India, China, Turkey and Persia. These were too costly for any but the very rich and were therefore often copied in embroidery or needlepoint. Needlepoint had the advantage of being thick as well as hardwearing and the pieces could be used as draught-excluders in the cold north or as protection from the heat of the sun in the south.

In the nineteenth century in Europe the designs became increasingly intricate – Germany and France favoured classical styles with figures, nymphs and shepherds, whereas the Dutch worked hangings showing everyday life such as market scenes. During this century the craft gained widespread popularity due to the introduction of Berlin woolwork. In 1810 the Berlin print seller Wittich produced a series of colour patterns based on famous paintings. These were instantly popular and at the same time the materials available improved with the introduction of high-quality and well dyed wool.

Art Nouveau designs were popular, and at the end of the nineteenth century William Morris's patterns spread throughout Europe and later to America. Even today these designs can be found in a vast range of kits. They adapt particularly well to needlepoint and can look as beautiful and appropriate today as they did a hundred years ago.

In the twentieth century the craft lost some of its popularity in Europe and America, particularly during the inter-war period when knitting took over as the most useful and functional pastime. It was only in the 1960s that there was a resurgence of interest in needlepoint when new designers emerged and the craft regained its former popularity.

Plain or basic needlepoint

The term needlepoint means stitching with wool onto canvas. Canvas is made of horizontal and vertical threads woven in a way that produces evenly spaced holes through which the wool is passed to produce each stitch. Unlike embroidery, the stitches in needlepoint can go only horizontally, vertically or diagonally in line with the holes in the canvas. At first this may seem limiting, but the types of wool and canvas available allow for great diversity and creativity. In many ways needlepoint is much simpler than embroidery as the canvas is fairly firm and you are less likely to make mistakes when positioning the stitches. It also tends to be quicker to cover an area of canvas,

which makes it very satisfying. This is particularly true with the coarser canvases. Unlike some embroidery and cross stitch patterns, needlepoint covers the entire canvas, giving a lovely rich feel to the finished piece.

This chapter covers the basic instructions and introduces the two main techniques: tent stitch and cross stitch. Both are very simple to master. The patterns produced are based on colour rather than on interesting variation in your stitching.

Canvas

As explained in Chapter 1, canvases vary in size from 18# to 3#. Petitpoint is 16# or above; anything below this is referred to as grospoint. 10# canvas is a particularly good size as it can easily be worked in cross stitch with one strand of tapestry wool. It is fine enough to allow a good amount of detail and is also simple to work with, even if the light isn't all that good! Size 12# has the same advantages if you choose to work in tent stitch. For needlepoint, mono or interlocking canvas is most suitable as the fineness of double canvas is rarely needed. Also, because of its structure, double canvas is more difficult to count accurately!

Tapestry wool, crewel wool and Persian wool are all suitable for needlepoint, as explained earlier. Crewel and Persian wool are finer than tapestry wool, and the threads can easily be separated. The ability to separate strands of yarn gives great flexibility, in terms of using the yarn on different gauges of canvas and for using a variety of stitches on one canvas. It also makes it possible to mix your own colours by using two or three differently coloured strands threaded together in one needle. Some needleworkers also feel that the multiple strands of crewel and Persian wool allow the stitches to lie flatter on the canvas. To a great extent the type of wool you use will be governed by the size of the canvas you have chosen, but for many projects tapestry wool is the easiest and most effective type of wool to use – and as most brands come in over 400 colours, the need to mix colours rarely arises.

Stitches

There is an enormous range of needlework stitches to choose from, but in this chapter the projects are completed using tent stitch or cross stitch, as the emphasis is on colour and pattern rather than texture. Both stitches are quick and easy and give good even coverage over the canvas.

Tent stitch is slightly more economical to use and quicker to stitch. However, it can distort the canvas – in some cases drastically – and you *do* need to use a frame, and possibly also stretch the piece when you have finished it. This is explained in Chapter 7.

Cross stitch uses slightly more wool, but gives a richer, fuller coverage on the canvas. This is true no matter what gauge of canvas you use. The other advantage of cross stitch is that, if you use the method given here, the canvas will not distort at all and you will not need to use a frame or stretch the finished work. This makes the piece truly portable. In some cases the size of canvas you are using will determine the type of stitch – for example, 18# uses tent stitch and 5# needs cross stitch to give a good covering.

The length of yarn is most important and should not be more than 30" (75 cm) long. If you buy your wool in Appleton hanks, this is conveniently half the length of the loop so you can just cut the hank in two. If you buy your wool any other way, unwind it at the beginning and cut it into lengths. This is not wasteful as any wool left over will be ready for your next project. It is tempting to think that a longer length of wool will save time by avoiding casting on and off so often but in fact the reverse is true, as the wool frays and tends to knot.

When casting on and off *never* use knots as this makes the work uneven. For the first stitch keep about 2" (5 cm) of wool beneath the canvas and secure it in place with the first line of stitches. Once you have covered some of the canvas this starting length can be threaded along behind already completed stitches. As you get to the end of each piece of wool, pull it through to the back of the canvas and run it through the back of adjacent stitches. This will secure it properly and ensure that the stitches do not work loose.

Tent stitch

This can be worked using three different methods:

- half cross stitch
- continental tent stitch
- basketweave or diagonal tent stitch.

Half cross stitch

All methods of tent stitch produce a diagonal stitch on the front of the canvas covering one row. When using half cross stitch, the back of the canvas consists of a series of vertical stitches. This is a very economical method of stitching in terms of the amount of wool used, but the coverage is slightly thin and therefore not suitable for background or large areas of one colour, as the canvas may show through. Stitch from right to left.

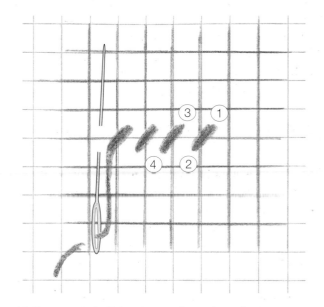

■ Half cross stitch. Bring the needle up from the back of the canvas (1) and insert it diagonally below (2). Bring the needle back through the canvas in the hole immediately above (3) ready to complete the next stitch (4).

■ Half cross stitch. When you reach the end of the row turn the canvas round and continue back in the opposite direction.

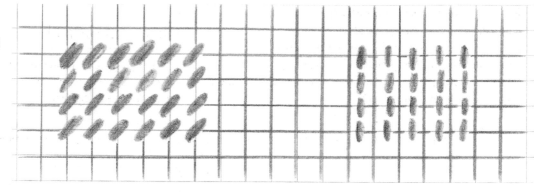

front   reverse

Continental tent stitch
This covers a larger area of canvas at the back of the design and therefore gives a thicker and stronger feeling to the piece, which is likely also to be firmer and to wear rather better. It is a very easy stitch, but it does use 30–40% more wool than half cross stitch.

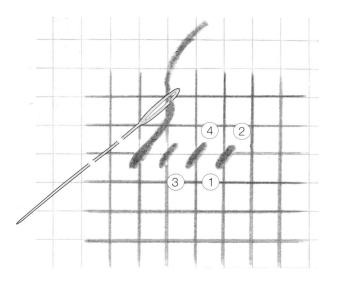

■ Continental tent stitch. Stitch from right to left. Bring the needle up from the back of the canvas (1) and insert it diagonally above (2). Bring the needle back through the canvas diagonally below and one stitch along (3), ready to complete the next stitch (4). When you reach the end of the row, turn the canvas round and continue in the opposite direction.

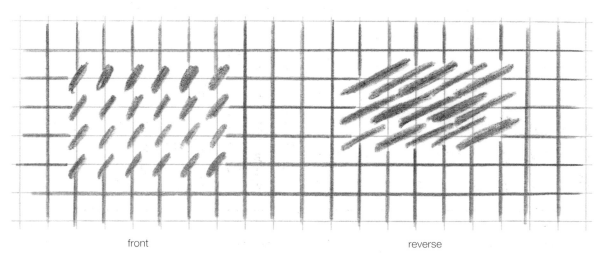

front   reverse

Basketweave or diagonal tent stitch

This stitch is especially suitable for large areas as it gives good coverage and distorts the canvas much less than the other two methods. The front of the canvas looks the same, but the back has a woven appearance – hence the name of the stitch.

■ Basketweave or diagonal tent stitch. These stitches are worked diagonally, coming up through (1), down through (2), up through (3) and down through (4). When you change direction, check the back of the canvas to make sure you are producing the basketweave pattern correctly.

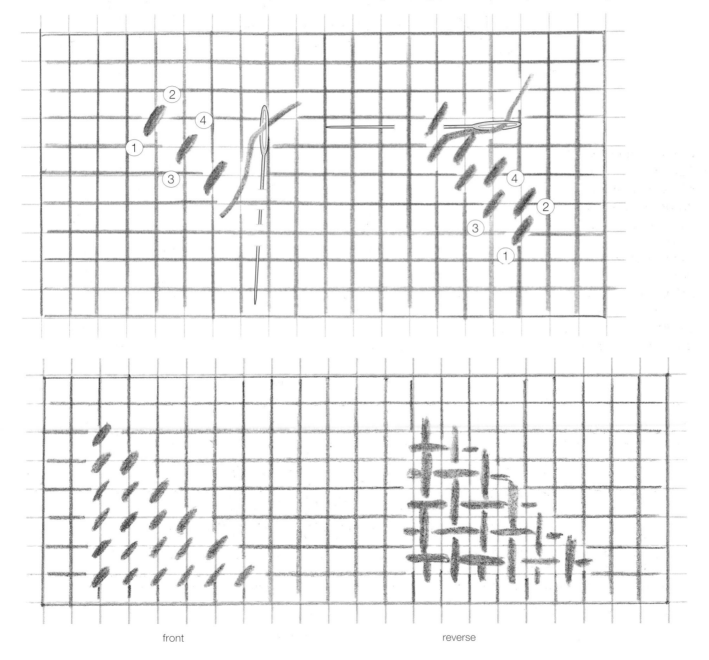

front   reverse

Cross stitch

There are various methods for producing this stitch, but the following one will not distort the canvas and will give even stitches. Each stitch should be completed individually. The rule to remember is that the wool on top of the canvas should travel diagonally, and that behind the canvas it should go either vertically or horizontally. This creates an even tension in all directions and avoids distortion.

Note that the needle always travels parallel to the canvas and not diagonally. This is particularly important when changing direction. Make sure that all your top stitches are facing the same way. This may sound obvious but it is easy to go wrong if you are filling in a complicated area and keep having to change direction.

If you are stitching a diagonal line or changing direction you need to position the needle carefully when completing the previous stitch so that when you move on the wool on the reverse of the canvas is still travelling either vertically or horizontally. It doesn't matter if you go diagonally on the reverse occasionally, but the more you do the more likely it is that the work will distort and need stretching back into shape.

Tension

This is how tightly or loosely you stitch. You should keep your tension as even as possible throughout or your work is likely to distort. If your tension is too tight, it will pull the canvas threads, making the canvas pucker. If the tension is too loose, you will end up with loops of wool and the stitches will not look neat. This is very important on large areas of the same colour where irregularities are most likely to show up. When filling in a background area remember to stitch straight across the canvas; if you complete such areas in blocks, it is likely to end up looking uneven. If you change direction at the point on the canvas where the pattern changes colour then the irregularity of the stitch will not show up. This may sound complicated, but most people develop an even tension automatically.

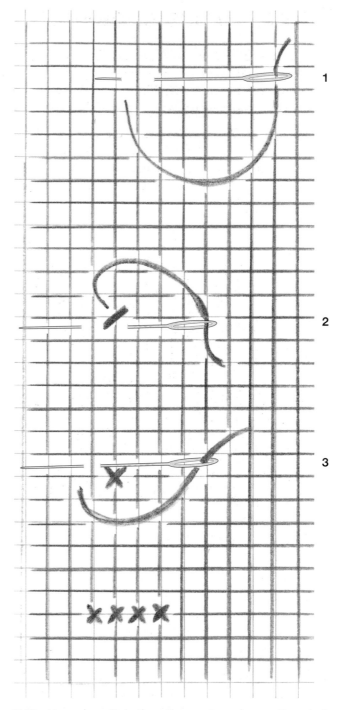

■ Working cross stitch. Pass the needle under one thread of canvas (1), complete that stitch (2), and pass the needle under two threads of canvas ready to make the next stitch (3).

Charts versus printed canvas

Many people think that charts are too difficult to follow, but once you have used one you will find that they are actually very easy. With charts you always know exactly where each colour should go, avoiding the frequent problem encountered on printed canvases where one stitch falls between two colours.

■ One square on the chart corresponds to one stitch.

Each square on the chart represents one stitch on the canvas. As each stitch is worked over the thread of the canvas, remember to count the intersections of thread, and not the holes in the canvas. Charts enable you to design your own patterns or adapt any other pattern.

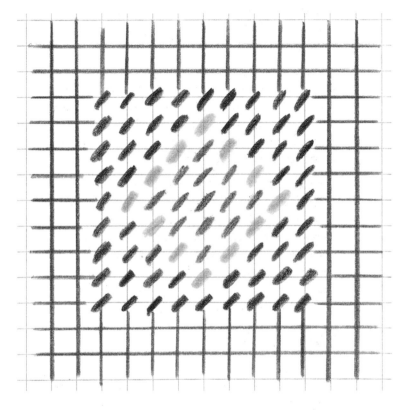

Getting started

First ensure that your piece of canvas is large enough for the project. It is very easy to cut off spare canvas at the end, and though this seems wasteful it is far easier than having to join an extra piece of canvas onto your work in order to finish it off.

Ideally 2–3" (5–7 cm) of canvas should be left around each edge of the design. It is possible to leave as little as 1" (2.5 cm), but this is risky unless you position the design very carefully. Leaving a large border of spare canvas has two main advantages:

■ If you do find that you misposition the pattern, you are less likely to go over the edge of the canvas.
■ It gives you leeway to enlarge the piece by adding another border, or to adapt the design as you see fit.

Having cut the canvas you need to bind the edges, as they are rough and will catch on the wool, causing it to fray. It is possible to do this with masking tape, though this can become unstuck with time and wear. It is better to stitch binding tape round the edges of your canvas. Place the binding tape over the edge of the canvas so that half is above and half below. Then tack round, ensuring both sides of the tape are attached to the canvas. Fold the tape over at an angle at the corners to ensure complete coverage. The stiff canvas will now have a frame of soft cotton, which will protect the wool and stop the canvas from fraying.

All canvases are stiff to begin with. They can be rinsed to remove some of the starch, but if you are going to join two pieces of canvas, or make a set (of cushions or mats, for instance), then make sure you rinse all the pieces of canvas at the same time. I find rinsing is not really necessary. If you store the canvas rolled up when you are not working on it, you will find that it soon softens. Remember not to fold your tapestry as this creates uneven pressure on some parts of the canvas, which leads to distortion.

When starting to work from a chart, it is usually best to stitch the general outline of the pattern first. Fold the canvas into quarters to find the centrepoint and work outwards from there. At the start it is *vital* to count correctly because any mistake will distort the whole pattern. Once you have stitched the basic outlines small mistakes may not matter, depending on the pattern. But at the beginning you must be prepared to count, count and count again. I know this sounds time-consuming (and of course it is), but once the basic outlines of your pattern are in place the rest becomes easy. At this stage it is also easy to unpick mistakes caused by bad counting, but as soon as other colours are involved it is much more difficult.

Changing a design

The colour of a design can be changed entirely to suit your taste, the only limit being your imagination and the availability of wool. The size and design may also be changed in one of two ways.

The first of these is to change the gauge of the canvas that you are using, which will increase or decrease the size of the whole piece. To work out the size of a piece, divide the number of stitches on the chart by the gauge size of the canvas – for example, 120 stitches on the chart worked on 10 count canvas = 12" (30 cm), 120 stitches on the chart worked on 5 count canvas = 24" (60 cm), 120 stitches on the chart worked on 6 count canvas = 20" (50 cm).

You will also need to adjust the amount of wool and possibly the needle size as well. The chart gives you a rough guide, but it will depend to some extent on how tightly you stitch. The basic rule is that one strand of tapestry wool = two strands of Persian wool = three strands of crewel wool.

Type of wool and number of strands

Canvas	Needle	Tent	Cross
5	16		3 Tapestry
7	16	5 Persian	2 Tapestry
10	18	3 Persian	1 Tapestry
		4 Crewel	2 Persian
			3 Crewel
12	18	1 Tapestry	1 Persian
		2 Persian	
		3 Crewel	
14	20	1 Tapestry	
		2 Persian	
		3 Crewel	
18	22	2 Crewel	

Repeating or leaving out part of the design can also change the size and shape of the finished piece. This will obviously change the amount of wool you need, and affect other parts of the design. For instance, the border may need to be changed to fit around the new central shape.

If you do make a mistake...

There will almost inevitably come a time when you make a mistake that needs correcting. This is particularly so in the outlines of patterns as they determine the shape of the entire design. If the mistake only involves a couple of stitches, it is perfectly possible to stitch over in the right colour. Stitch loosely so that the bottom colour does not show through. For larger areas that have gone wrong, it will unfortunately be necessary to unpick the stitches.

Never cut the wool unless you are absolutely certain that it is the right thread. It is much safer to unpick the stitches with a needle rather than cutting through them, even though this seems very laborious. This way you avoid the worse danger of cutting through the canvas itself. It is easiest to unpick the stitches in the reverse direction to the order in which they were sewn – i.e. unpick the last stitch first. Once you have unpicked all the stitches, remove all the wool fibres from the canvas because they could show through the next colour. Remember that you must unpick all the stitches completed with the strand of wool and not just those that are incorrect – if you leave some, they will unravel.

Project 1 · Indian parrot and elephant cushion

This pattern is one traditionally used for the fine ikat-woven patolu saris of Gujerat and Andra Pradesh where some of the weaving techniques have overlapped the state borders. In Gujerat this particular pattern is called *popat kunjar bhat* (parrot and elephant pattern) and tends to be used only on the finest ceremonial saris. At Jampath in New Delhi there are state emporiums which show the crafts of all the regions of India. They are, of course, primarily aimed at the tourist market but even so good pieces can be found and beautiful silk woven saris in this pattern can often be seen.

■ The completed cushion.

Equipment needed

- 10# interlocking canvas 20" (50 cm) square
- Fabric for the back of the cushion 18" (45 cm) square
- Tapestry needle size 18
- Appleton tapestry wool:
- Green   529   one hank
- Brown   587   two and a half hanks
- Red   504   two and a half hanks
- Yellow   556   two skeins
- Orange   994   one hank
- Beige   181   one and a half hanks

Working the design

This pattern is worked in cross stitch and should not need a frame to prevent it distorting. To start, prepare the canvas as described earlier. Fold the canvas in quarters to find the centre and stitch the outlines of the diamonds. At this point it is very important to position the stitches correctly. Once you have the outlines it is much easier to complete the rest of the pattern. Complete the pattern up to the final two red lines of stitching and sew these through both layers of canvas, as described in the finishing instructions (Chapter 7). Complete the border in red wool and trim the unused canvas.

The finished cushion is about 15" (38 cm) square. The size of cushion pad is a matter of personal preference. A 15" (38 cm) pad will leave the cushion soft and loose, whereas a 16" (40 cm) one will result in a firmer, more solid cushion.

■ Chart for the parrot and elephant cushion.

Project 2 · Persian pattern

This pattern comes from a large bag I bought in an antique shop in South-west England. Originally it came from the inhospitable region of Kerman in South-east Iran, where it was made by the Afshar, a nomadic tribe which settled there. Traditionally the area was used as a place of exile for politically troublesome or dangerous tribes, but now the inhabitants are peacefully settled, many even

abandoning their nomadic way of life. Those that do still migrate spend the summers living in large black tents which dot the landscape, and it is in one of these tents that this bag would probably have been used to store the family's belongings.

The pattern is easily adapted and I have used it for a rug, needlecase and cheque book cover. If you wished to make a cushion or even a large bag similar to the original, it would be simple to do so by repeating the pattern several times.

■ Left: The Persian pattern can be adapted in any number of ways, only four of which are given here.

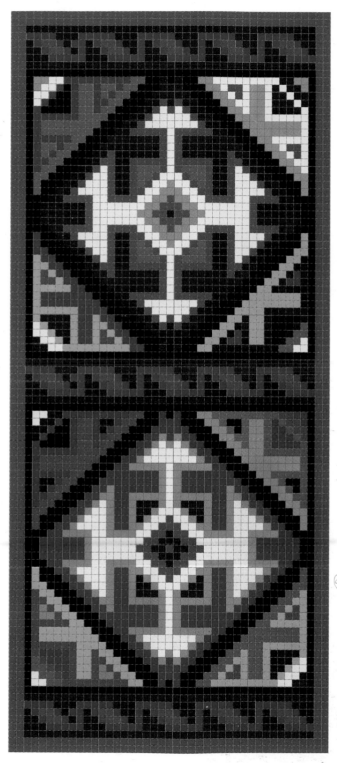

Equipment needed

Rug
- 6# interlocking single canvas 13" × 23" (33 × 58 cm)
- Tapestry needle size 16
- Backing fabric 21" × 11" (53 × 28 cm) (optional)
- Wool for tassels
- Appleton tapestry wool in the quantities given in the chart. For the rugs the stitches are worked with two strands of wool to cover the canvas fully.

Needlecase
- 10# interlocking single canvas 14" × 7" (35 × 18 cm)
- Tapestry needle size 18
- Lining fabric 11" × 6" (28 × 15 cm)
- Piece of felt 10" (25 cm) square for pages
- Button for fastening
- Appleton tapestry wool in quantities given in the chart

Cheque book cover
- 10# interlocking single canvas 21" × 7" (53 × 18 cm)
- Tapestry needle size 18
- Lining fabric: two pieces each 9" × 5" (23 × 13 cm)
- Appleton tapestry wool in the quantities given in the chart

Persian pattern project: quantities needed

	Blue Rug	Brown Rug	Needlecase	Cheque Book Cover
■ Brown 187	1½ hanks	1½ hanks	½ hank	½ hank
■ Mid Brown 974 (grey)	½ hank	1½ hanks	2 skeins	2 skeins
■ Mustard 765	½ hank	1½ hanks	2 skeins	1 skein
■ Fawn 981	½ hank	½ hank	2 skeins	1 skein
■ Navy 852	1 hank	1 hank	½ hank	2 skeins
■ Turquoise 565	1 hank	1 skein	2 skeins	1 skein
■ Red 225	1½ hanks	1 hank	½ hank	2 skeins
■ Pink 223	½ hank	½ hank	2 skeins	1 skein

■ Persian pattern – chart for needlecase.

Working the designs

These patterns are worked in cross stitch and should not need the use of a frame. For all the projects, prepare the canvas as described earlier and then fold in quarters to find the centre. It is easiest to stitch the navy blue outlines first and then complete the individual patterns. In all cases stitch up to the two outer rows through two layers of canvas as described in the finishing instructions. Follow the instructions given on pages 102–103 to complete the project.

centre line

centre line

■ Persian pattern – the cheque book cover.

■ Persian pattern – brown rug.   ■ Persian pattern – blue rug.

5

Bargello

Bargello has a complicated history and is referred to in a great many different ways, but it is actually a very straightforward method of stitching. It is usually worked in wool on canvas and consists of a series of vertical stitches. At its simplest it can be any design worked in straight stitches but traditionally particular designs have become associated with it.

Bargello is frequently called *Florentine work* or *Hungarian point*, but these names refer to types of stitches rather than the designs as a whole. In Florentine work all the stitches are the same length, whereas with Hungarian point this length can vary. Other names you may meet associated with this stitching are Irish, flame, brick, zick-zack or cushion, all of which refer to the same type of stitching.

There are a number of romantic stories regarding the origins of this work, all equally plausible. In 895 Hungary was invaded by Magyars, who brought the designs and needlework traditions of the Eastern Steppes with them. As the inhabitants of Hungary developed a more settled lifestyle, needlework of all types flourished. In 1383 King Vladislav V of Poland married Princess Jadwiga of Hungary. Although she was only thirteen, Jadwiga was an accomplished needlewoman and stitched many works for the court and crown in Hungarian point. This type of stitching became popular throughout the country and was often referred to as Bargello after Vladislav's family name – Jagiello.

■ Top right: Persian pattern: brown rug

The second story involves King Corvinus I (Matthias) who ruled Hungary between 1458 and 1490. He spent much time in France and Italy and was sufficiently influenced by the Renaissance to set up a cultural centre in Budapest. Italian artists were established there and encouraged to combine Hungarian tradition with Italian techniques. Textiles in particular flourished during this period and Hungarian point and Florentine work became widely known throughout Europe.

Another possible origin of the name is the Florentine Bargello Palace, which was built by the noble Podesta family. By the sixteenth century it was the residence of the chief of police and was occupied by political prisoners condemned to die. Needlework was introduced as a form of therapy for the prisoners and when the building was renovated in 1865 and turned into a museum the inventory listed several chairs worked in this method.

Whatever its origins, Bargello became a popular type of stitchery and spread widely, absorbing stitches and designs from many countries. In Florence and Elizabethan England silks were often used and an inventory of 1600 describes the colours as 'Carnacon pinks, Marigolde-colour, purples, blews, straw-colour, Murrey, Ladie-blush and pounde-cythrone colour.' The Scots used tartan wool to create hardwearing pieces in soft, muted colours and in the eighteenth century the technique spread to North America. Here Bargello was particularly popular with the colonists as the designs were not realistic and therefore did not require the use of particular colours – for example, blue for the sky. The early colonists had to be very thrifty in order to survive and the patterns of Bargello enabled them to use whatever colours they had to hand. Gradually, as life became easier, the patterns became more ornate.

Materials

Canvas

Bargello should be worked on single-thread (mono) or interlocking canvas. The latter is preferable if you can get it as it holds its shape better. Double canvas (Penelope) is not suitable as it makes the stitches more complicated to work.

Yarn

Bargello can be worked in anything from fine stranded cotton to tapestry wool. What is important is that the thread should completely cover the canvas so that none of the canvas shows through the stitches when the piece is finished. Canvas sizes between 10# and 18# are the most suitable and the chart below shows the quantities of thread or wool needed to give a good coverage.

■ Left: Cushion worked in Bargello, dating from the 17th century.

Needles

Tapestry needles should be used. The relevant sizes are given in the chart below.

Yarns and needles for Bargello work

Canvas size	Needle	Tapestry	Persian	Crewel	Stranded cotton
10#	18	2	4	5	
12#	18	2	3		
14#	20/18		2	4	
16#	20	1	2		
18#	22	1		3	6

Charts

Each line on the chart represents a single thread on the canvas (either horizontal or vertical). The pattern consists of vertical lines on the chart, which indicate how many horizontal threads each stitch should cover. Different colours of wool can be indicated by various colours on the chart or different types of line.

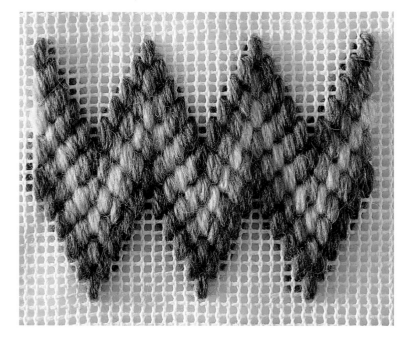

■ Stitched sample.

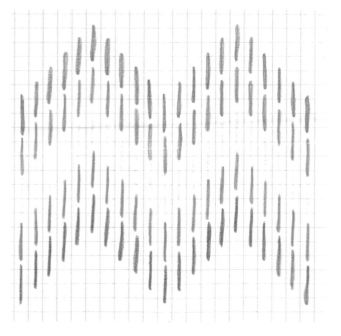

■ Chart of central area. On a chart, the stitches are shown in different colours or different types of line.

Stitches

The stitches can be worked in two ways. The first is very economical in the amount of wool used, but results in a slightly thin covering. Bring the needle up through the canvas at the bottom of the stitch. Pass it back through the canvas at the top of the stitch and then travel diagonally behind the canvas to bring the wool up through at the top of the next stitch. In this method the stitches are worked up and down alternately and the reverse of the canvas has small diagonal stitches which form the steps between the verticals.

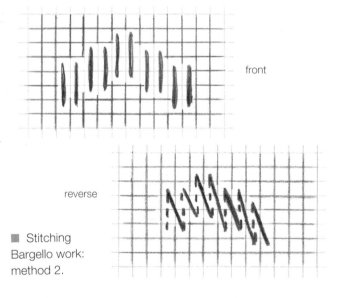

front

reverse

■ Stitching Bargello work: method 2.

The second method uses more wool at it passes behind the whole length of the previous stitch but it provides a richer, thicker look and is usually more satisfactory. For this method all the stitches are worked from the bottom upwards. Bring the needle up through the canvas at the bottom of the stitch. Pass it back through the canvas at the top of the stitch and then pass it diagonally across the back of the canvas to come up at the bottom of the next stitch. This results in more wool at the back of the canvas than at the front, but strengthens the work and usually looks much better.

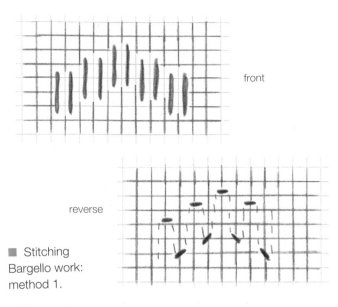

front

reverse

■ Stitching Bargello work: method 1.

All Bargello patterns are created by stitching one or other of the above methods. The stitches are worked horizontally across the canvas using steps to create the diagonal effect. Each step refers to the number of horizontal threads between the bottom of one stitch and the next one. There are many variations possible, but the distance of the step must always be less than the length of the stitch – for example, if your stitches cover four horizontal threads, the steps cannot be more than three threads. This can be written as two numbers separated by a full stop – for example, 3.2 – the first number representing the stitch size and the second number the step. Stitches can be anything between two and nine threads long.

Although all stitches are worked in the same way, many patterns have individual names. The basic ones are shown in the diagrams. These can be combined in almost any way to give a limitless number of variations.

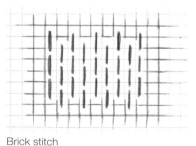

■ Variations that can be achieved using the basic stitches.

Brick stitch

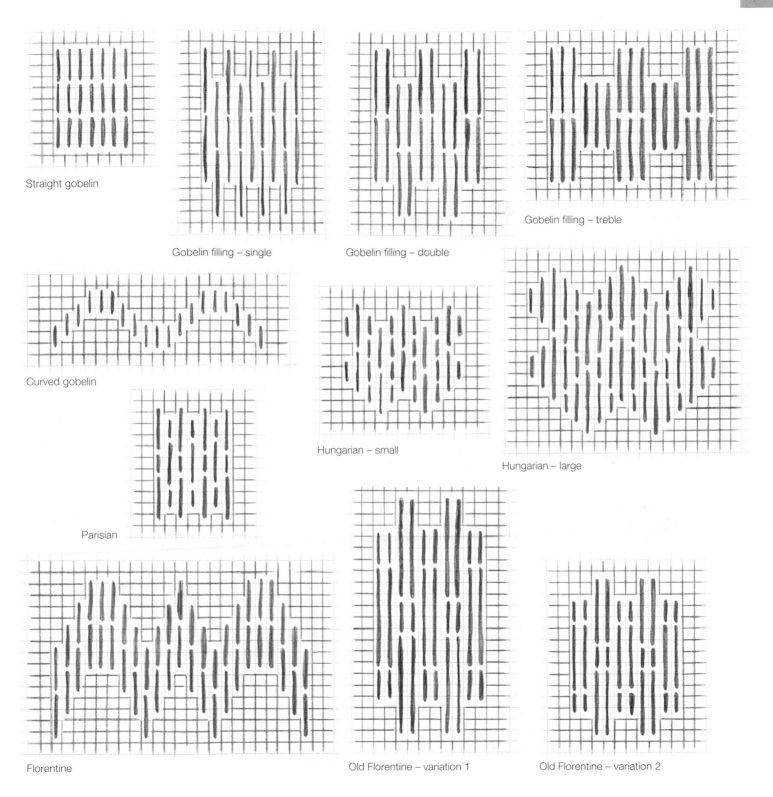

Straight gobelin

Gobelin filling – single

Gobelin filling – double

Gobelin filling – treble

Curved gobelin

Hungarian – small

Hungarian – large

Parisian

Florentine

Old Florentine – variation 1

Old Florentine – variation 2

Brick stitch Each stitch is two threads long and each step is one stitch.

Straight Gobelin These stitches can be any length and form uniform straight lines across the canvas. They are useful at the top and bottom of patterns in Bargello as they can be used to create curves.

Gobelin filling This is similar to brick stitch, except here the stitches are six threads long and the steps three. There are several variations of Gobelin filling, two of which are shown in the figure.

Florentine stitch Florentine stitches can be any length, but within a piece of work their size must be uniform.

Hungarian stitch (Hungarian point) This stitch produces a pattern of small diamonds, each of which consists of three stitches. The stitch can be adapted to create larger diamonds by using five stitches.

Parisian stitch The pattern consists of alternate long and short stitches. It creates an irregular texture across the canvas.

Old Florentine This is similar to Parisian except the stitches are worked in pairs and are longer. Various sizes of old Florentine are shown in the figure.

Tension

Bargello stitches are usually quite long, covering two to nine threads of the canvas, and because of this it is very easy to pull the threads too tight and distort the canvas. Unless you stitch very evenly or the piece of work is small, it is often much easier to work on a frame. This keeps the canvas firm while you are stitching and avoids the need for stretching when you have finished.

The canvas should be attached to the frame vertically – i.e. at the top and bottom – as the stitches only pull vertically and the canvas is unlikely to distort horizontally.

Starting

As always, ensure you have sufficient canvas for the pattern you want to stitch. Unless you are very sure of yourself, leave a good 2" (5 cm) on all sides. If you are using a frame, the top and bottom of the canvas will be fixed to it so only the sides need to be bound. Stitch the binding over the two sides, ensuring the edges are completely covered. Place the binding tape over the edge of the canvas so that half is above and half below. Then tack in place, ensuring both sides of the tape are attached to the canvas. If you are not using a frame, bind all four edges of the canvas.

Where you start stitching is down to personal preference and may be dictated by the pattern you have chosen. If the pattern is repeated in a line across the canvas, it is best to stitch a single line right across and then work out from there. If the design consists of a repeated pattern, then it is usually best to stitch the outline first.

At this point it is *very* important to make sure that all the stitches are exactly the right size and in the right place. In some patterns mistakes may not show once you have stitched the outline, but any mistakes at the beginning will distort the whole pattern. At this stage you must check, check and check again. This is obviously time-consuming, but once the basic pattern is established the rest is easy. At this stage it is easy to unpick mistakes, but once large areas are stitched this becomes much more difficult.

Designs

The designs in Bargello are geometric rather than pictorial. The pattern is usually fairly simple and the overall design is created by repetitions of this pattern, usually exactly, or sometimes in varying colours. According to which colours are used the effect can be dramatic or gentle. Although they vary in length and position, the stitches are all the same shape and because of this the colour is particularly important in Bargello. A colour wheel (see below) is useful for determining effects – for example, colours close to each other, such as blues and greens, are harmonious whereas opposites (such as blue and yellow) will provide a contrast. Dark and light shades of the same colour will also provide a contrast, with the light colour standing out and the dark shade being less dominant. As a rule, reds, oranges and yellows tend to stand out more than greens, blues and violets.

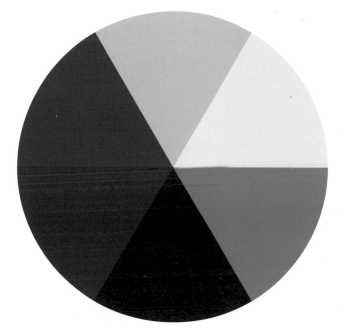

■ The colour wheel can be of great use when planning your design.

Apart from colour, the design is also influenced by the way in which the pattern is repeated.

Row repeats

The pattern is based on a single row going right across the canvas from one side to the other. This line is then repeated in a sequence of colours which form the pattern unit. Anything from three colours upwards may be used. This pattern is then repeated up and down the canvas.

Motif repeats

The pattern is mirrored vertically – the top half and bottom half are identical images of each other. This pattern then repeats across and up and down the canvas. Patterns can vary from simple diamonds to complicated interlocking shapes.

Four-way repeat

This is an adaptation of Bargello in which the pattern radiates from a single point, each quarter being a mirror image of the quarters on either side. If you are going to design a pattern with this type of repeat it is much easier if you find the centre of the canvas by folding it in four and then marking the four quarters exactly with tacking thread.

row repeats

motif repeats

■ Repeating a pattern in different ways influences the design.

four-way repeat

Mistakes

As with needlepoint, be very careful before you cut any stitches which are incorrect. It is much safer to unpick them rather than risk cutting the wrong stitches or even the canvas itself. Follow the instructions given in Chapter 4.

Project 1 ·
Four-way pincushion

This attractive pincushion is worked on a four-way repeat and can be made into either a square or a circular cushion. If you choose the square pincushion, you will probably need to make the inner pad yourself and instructions for this are given on page 105. Ready-made circular bases are easily available, but remember that you should buy the pincushion before starting to stitch as sizes vary. Pincushions usually come on a removable base and are easily available from department stores or specialist needlecraft shops.

Equipment needed

- Pincushion (either made or bought)
- Paterna Persian wool, using two strands. One skein of each colour, as shown in the chart
- Tapestry needle size 20
- 14# interlocking canvas (or mono if you prefer) 9" × 9" (23 × 23 cm)

Colours for the four-way pincushion

Pink/blue colourway	Green/yellow colourway
■ Dark Blue 510	■ Dark Green 520
■ Mid Blue 512	■ Mid Green 521
■ Pale Blue 513	■ Pale Green 523
■ Dark Pink 911	■ Yellow 762
■ Pale Pink 912	■ Cream 764

Working the design

Prepare the canvas as described earlier. It is not necessary to use a frame for such a small project, so stitch binding tape round all four sides of the canvas.

Work the stitches from the centre outwards, following the chart. The stitch length varies so be very careful to make sure each one is the correct length. As the pattern is largely repetitive this becomes easier as you progress. On a piece this small it is best to complete all four quarters in each colour and then move on to the next colour rather than stitching each quarter individually.

The wool allowances are the same for either pincushion. If you are stitching the square one, work the pattern to the line indicated. The outer pattern will cover a round pincushion of 4" (10 cm) diameter, but check before you stitch it in place as some ready-made pincushions vary slightly. If necessary simply add extra stitches round the edge to cover any exposed areas of canvas.

When you have finished, press the canvas with a warm iron under a damp cloth. Unless you have stitched very tightly or unevenly, it will not need stretching. Then follow the making-up instructions on page 105.

■ Four-way pincushions.

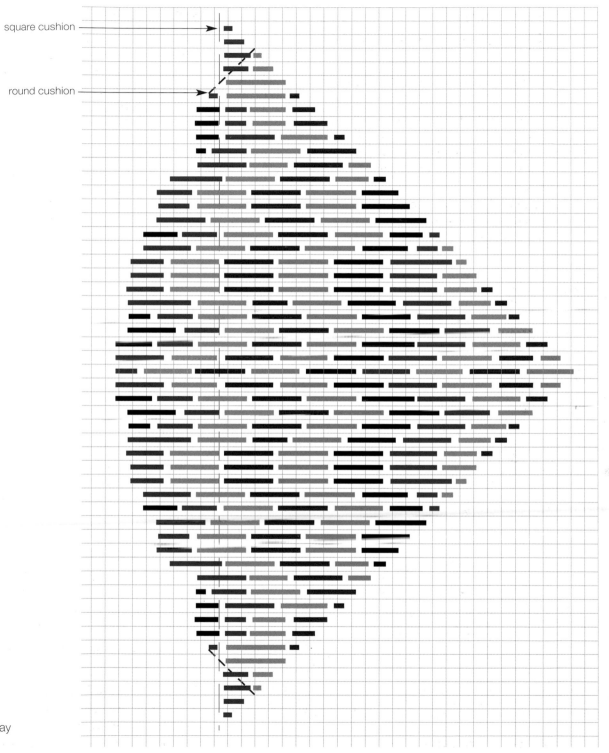

square cushion

round cushion

■ Chart for the four-way
pincushion.

Project 2 ·
Guatemalan purse

The pattern on this purse comes from Nebaj in the Quiché district of Guatemala. This particular design is very popular as the four geometric points are thought to symbolise the four cardinal points of the Earth. In Guatemala this design would be woven into strips and used to decorate clothes like a scarf or a head-dress. Although it is not a country associated with Bargello, this design can be adapted perfectly and stitched onto canvas.

The pattern can be repeated endlessly and if you wished you could work a larger piece of canvas and make a bag as well.

Equipment needed

- 16# mono canvas 13" × 16" (33 × 40 cm)
- Tapestry needle size 20
- Two buttons for fastening
- Lining fabric 11" × 14" (28 × 35 cm)
- Appleton tapestry wool:

■ Red	995	half a hank
■ Pink	145	half a hank
White	882	two skeins
■ Green	832	half a hank
■ Navy	747	half a hank
■ Turquoise	483	two skeins
Yellow	471	two skeins
■ Purple	606	two skeins
■ Orange	862	two skeins

■ Purse based on a pattern from Guatemala.

Working the design

Prepare the canvas as described earlier.
If you stitch fairly loosely and evenly you
will not need to use a frame, but if you
pull the stitches tightly you would be
better to use one as it will prevent the
canvas from puckering up. It is best to
complete the outsides of the diamonds
first. I usually stitch one row of diamonds
at a time, but the order you tackle the
project in is up to you because any way
would work as well as another.

When you have finished the diamonds,
stitch the seven rows as indicated at the
top and the bottom. Press the piece with
a warm iron under a damp cloth and
make up the bag as described on page 106.

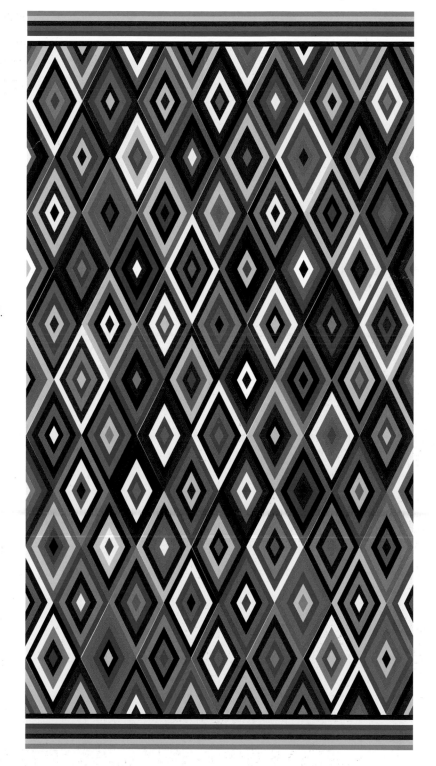

■ Colour chart for the Guatemalan purse.

bargello

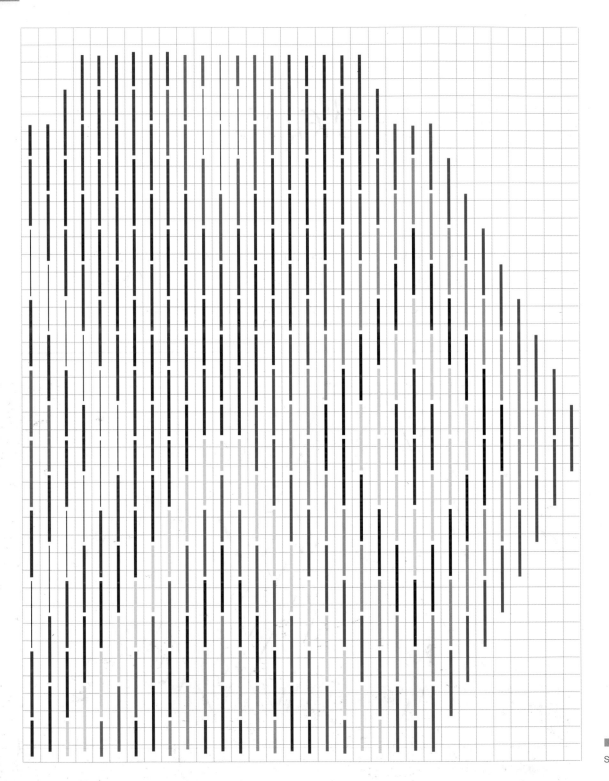

■ Guatemalan purse:
stitching chart.

6

Ornamental needlepoint

The term needlepoint is frequently used just to describe the stitches already covered, but in fact there is an enormous range of stitches which can be worked on canvas. With these stitches, variations in texture as well as colour can be achieved, thus widening the design possibilities greatly.

It is perfectly easy to invent your own stitches – any combination of working the wool through the canvas can be regarded as a stitch. However, there is a wide range of recognised stitches and it is probably easiest to start with these. They fall into four main groups: straight, diagonal, cross and composite, each term describing the main characteristic of the stitch. Most of the straight stitches are covered in Chapter 5, the others are described in the following section.

Straight stitches

Back stitch

This is a very useful stitch for pattern outlines or for separating two types of stitch. It can be worked over any number of threads and can travel in any direction on the canvas. This is particularly useful when outlining complicated shapes such as flowers. It is also useful for filling in gaps between stitches if any canvas shows through.

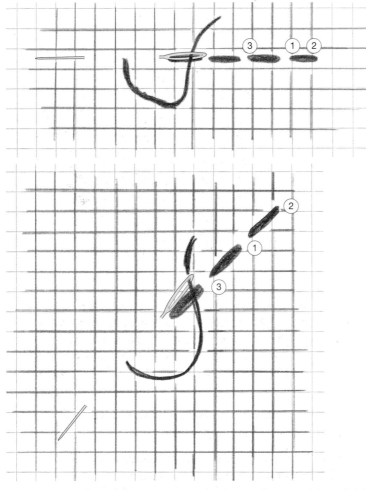

■ Back stitch. The stitches can be worked up or down and from the left or right. In all cases bring the wool up through the canvas at 1, back down through 2 and up again at 3. Always have the needle pointing in the direction in which you are stitching.

Satin stitch

This is another useful stitch, which can cover any number of threads and travel in any direction. Unlike back stitch, it is used for filling in areas of canvas and, within reason, the size of the stitch can be altered to fill in the available space. For large areas it is usually better to use two stitches or to divide the area with a row of back stitch as satin stitches covering more than six or seven threads of canvas do not always lie evenly.

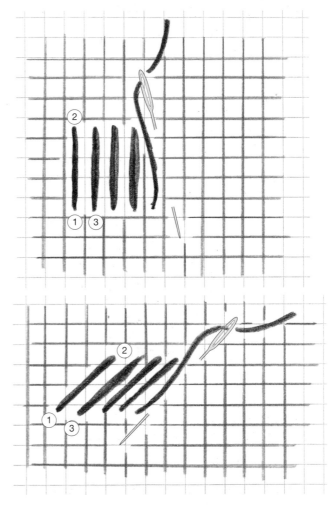

■ Satin stitch. Bring the wool up through the canvas at 1 and pass it down through 2. Then bring the wool up again through 3, being very careful not to pull the wool too tightly as this will cause the canvas to pucker. Continue placing each stitch exactly next to the previous one.

Diagonal stitches

The most well known diagonal stitch is tent or half cross stitch, which is described in Chapter 4.

■ Diagonal stitches – 1. All stitches are worked on 12# canvas with two strands of Persian wool. **1** Diagonal; **2** Byzantine; **3** Jacquard; **4** Chequer; **5** Scottish.

Diagonal stitch

This stitch can give a woven effect if it is worked in one colour or several similar shades. If it is worked in contrasting colours it will result in bold diagonal lines across the canvas. It forms a close covering over the canvas and is particularly suitable for chair covers or bags as it is hardwearing.

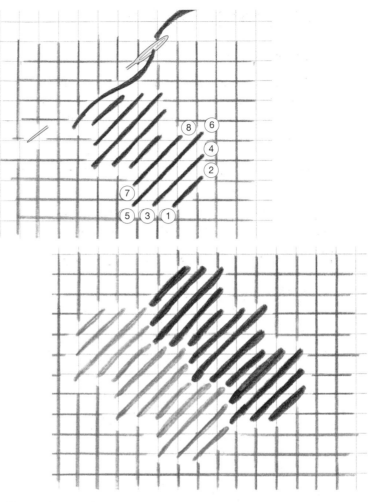

■ Diagonal stitch. Bring the wool up through the canvas at 1 and then pass it back down at 2 (two stitches away diagonally). The wool is brought up through 3 and down through 4 (three diagonals). Continue the pattern up through 5 and down through 6 (four diagonals). Finally bring the thread up through 7 and down through 8 (three diagonals).

The pattern is worked diagonally across the canvas and is made up of a four-stitch repeat.

You can work up or down across the canvas, providing all the stitches lie in the same direction. The next row is worked in exactly the same way as shown in the Figure, with the shortest stitch being placed on the same diagonal line as the previous row's largest stitch. This ensures that the rows fit together and cover the canvas completely.

Byzantine stitch

This stitch is worked diagonally over four vertical and horizontal threads or more. It creates a pattern of steps and is very useful for filling in background areas. If you wish to emphasize the steps do the rows in alternate colours.

If the diagonal steps do not exactly fill the required area, continue the pattern with smaller stitches. Do not change the step pattern as any irregularity in this will spoil the overall design. Variations can be achieved by altering either the size of the stitches or the size of the steps.

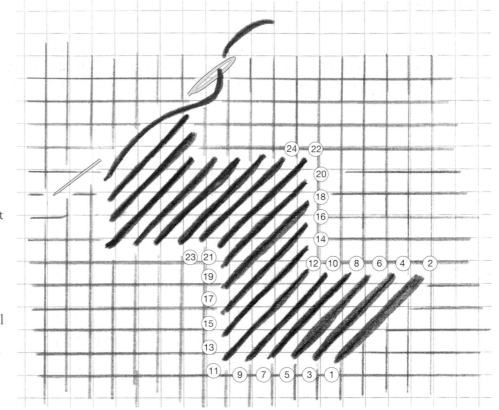

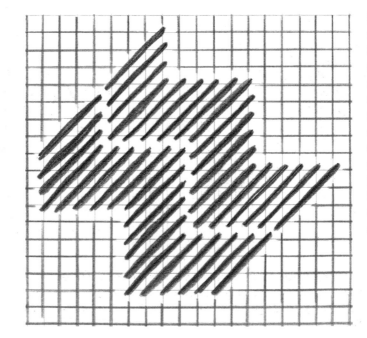

■ Byzantine stitch. Bring the wool up through 1 and pass it back down through the canvas at 2 (four stitches diagonally above). Continue as shown, taking the step upwards at 13–14. Then continue vertically until the step changes direction again at 23–24. Continue the pattern in this way across the canvas. The next row should fit immediately above or below the previous one.

Jacquard stitch

This is a similar stitch to Byzantine, but consists of two rows of steps: one small (worked over one diagonal intersection) and one larger (worked over two or more diagonal intersections). Each row should be completed before moving on to the next.

As with Byzantine stitch, if the pattern does not exactly fit into the area, alter the size of the stitches but do not alter the arrangement of steps. This stitch can be worked in one or more colours depending on the effect you wish to create.

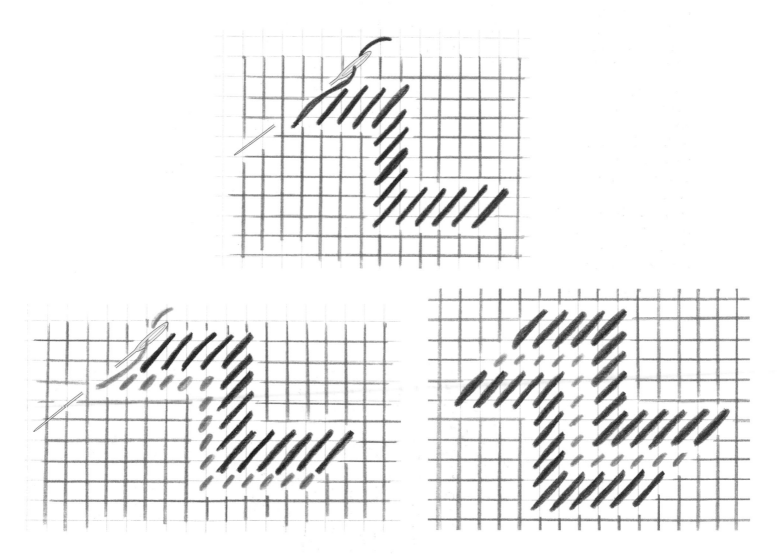

■ Working Jacquard stitch. Work the first row of steps as shown in the diagram, with each stitch covering two diagonal intersections. Then complete the next row following the pattern of steps, but with each stitch covering only one diagonal intersection. Continue the pattern in this way until the required area is filled.

Chequer stitch

This consists of alternating blocks of diagonal stitch and tent stitch. Each square covers four diagonal and four horizontal threads of the canvas. It is often worked in a single colour as this produces an interesting texture, but can also be used to create a chequerboard effect (hence its name) by using two contrasting colours.

Whether you work diagonally, horizontally or vertically in rows is up to you, but if you are using contrasting colours it would probably be easier to complete all the blocks of one colour. If you are doing this, ensure that you position the blocks correctly and count the stitches accurately as otherwise the pattern can very easily distort.

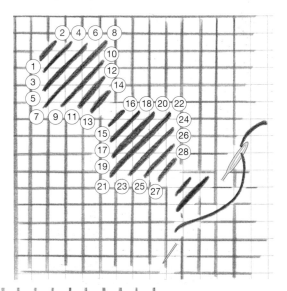

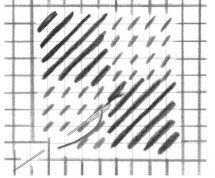

■ Chequer stitch. The first block should be worked following numbers 1–14. The next square can then be completed diagonally below this following numbers 15–28. The remaining blocks should then be filled in with tent stitch over one diagonal intersection as shown.

Scottish stitch

This is a combination of diagonal stitch and tent stitch. The diagonal stitches are worked into square blocks, which are then separated by tent stitches worked over one diagonal intersection. It creates a cushioned effect as the squares stand out from the dividing lines of tent stitch.

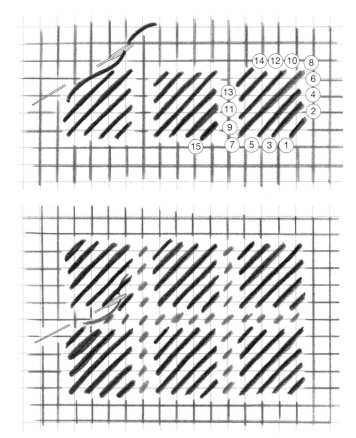

■ Scottish stitch is a combination of diagonal stitch and tent stitch. Form the first cushion block by stitching 1–14 as shown in the diagram. The stitches are worked over 1,2,3,4,3,2,1 intersections, respectively. Repeat this pattern horizontally and vertically across the canvas, leaving one line of intersections between each square. These lines should then be worked in tent stitch. The size of the squares can be varied by changing the number of stitches – e.g. 1,2,3,2,1 or 1,2,3,4,5,4,3,2,1.

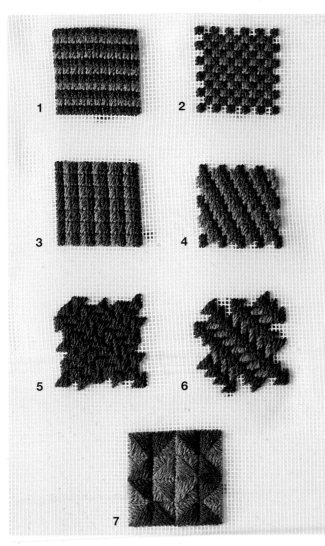

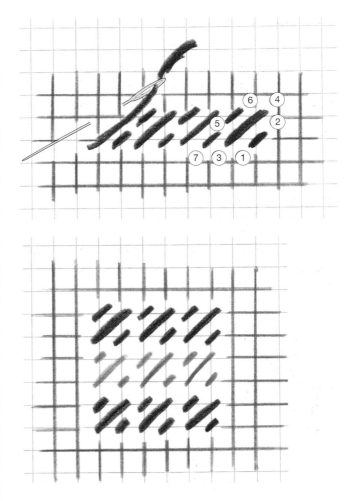

■ Diagonal stitches – 2. All stitches are worked on 12# canvas with two strands of Persian wool. **1** Mosaic; **2** Mosaic variation; **3** Cashmere; **4** Cashmere variation; **5** Milanese; **6** Oriental; **7** Cross-cornered cushion.

■ Mosaic stitch. To work the pattern horizontally, stitch 1–6 in the diagram. This creates the basic stitch and consists of three diagonal stitches worked over 1,2,1 diagonal intersections. Begin the next stitch diagonally below the last stitch of the previous block (7). Continue along the row repeating the 1,2,1 pattern.

Mosaic stitch

This stitch consists of blocks of three diagonal stitches which can be worked horizontally or diagonally across the canvas. The name comes from the intricate patterns that can be created if more than one colour is used. If you are only using one colour, the effect will be the same whether you work horizontally or diagonally.

To work the pattern diagonally, stitch the first block as described above. Work the first stitch of the second block diagonally above the last stitch of the previous block. The first block is numbers 1–6 and the second block is numbers 7–12, as shown in the figure on page 80. This stitch can be worked diagonally up or down the canvas.

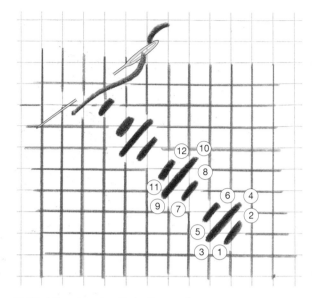
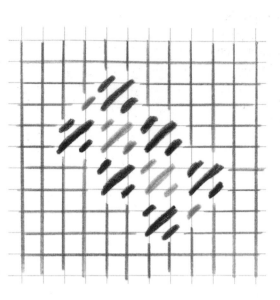

■ Working mosaic stitch diagonally.

Cashmere stitch

This stitch is similar to mosaic in that the pattern is formed of blocks but in this case the blocks are rectangular rather than square.

1

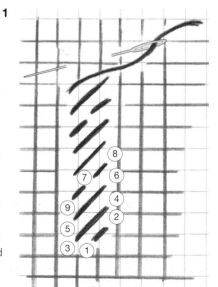

■ Cashmere stitch. The first block should be worked completing stitches 1–8. The second block is level with the first and is worked in the same way beginning at 9. When you have completed the row, you can turn the canvas round and work your way back in the same way.

2

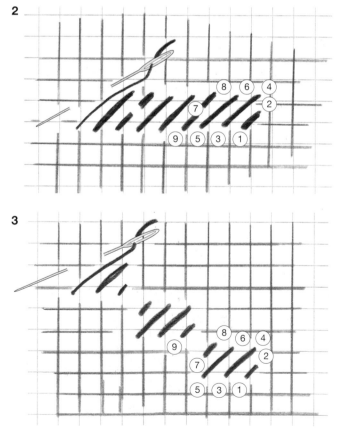

3

You can either align the blocks exactly to form a grid pattern or start each stitch one row further over, thereby producing a staggered effect, as shown in the diagram.

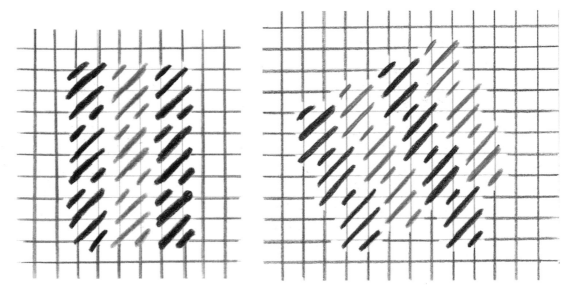

■ Cashmere stitches can be worked straight or staggered.

Cashmere – straight

Cashmere – staggered

Milanese stitch

This stitch and its variation, Oriental stitch, form large dramatic patterns. They consist of the same basic shape, a triangle formed by decreasing diagonal stitches. If worked in one colour this will create a series of large steps across the canvas.

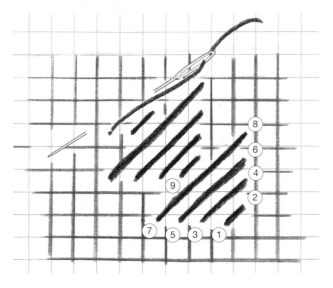

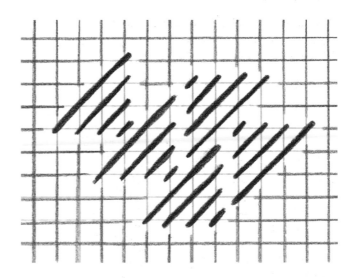

■ Milanese stitch. For Milanese stitch work a triangle diagonally on the canvas following numbers 1–8. Then bring the needle up through the canvas at 9 and continue the pattern. When you have finished the triangles work your way back up the canvas, stitching the triangles in reverse so they fit exactly into the previous row.

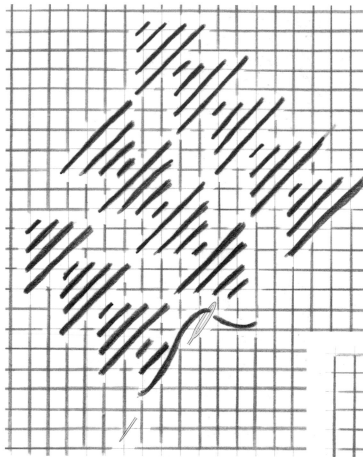

The first set of triangles is worked in the same way for Oriental stitch, but the second returning rows are placed further away to allow a row of diagonal stitches to be placed in between each triangle. Having completed the first row of triangles, continue back up the canvas but position the triangles so that the longest stitch of each one is diagonally aligned with the largest stitch of the triangle in the previous row. When you have finished all the triangles, you can then fill in the diagonal stitches between the triangles, each area consisting of three stitches worked over two diagonal intersections as shown below. If you work this pattern in one colour, it will result in large steps across the canvas, but if you use a different colour for the infilling, a series of arrowheads will develop.

■ Oriental stitch is a variation of Milanese stitch.

Cross-cornered cushion stitch

This stitch consists of a diagonally worked square, part of which is then stitched over in the opposite direction.

The pattern in the photograph below has been repeated four times to form a central diamond, but it can be used in many ways to form many different patterns. The upper stitches can also be worked in a different colour to create interesting effects.

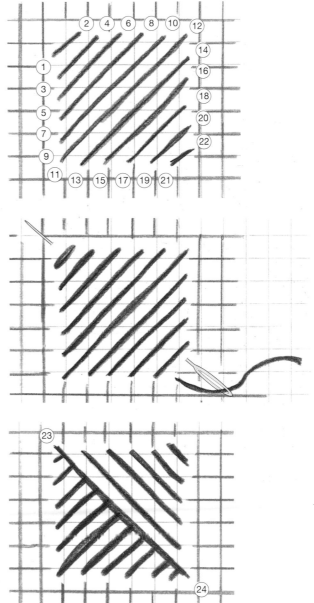

■ Working cross-cornered cushion stitch. Work the square following numbers 1–22. This consists of a series of graduating diagonal stitches increasing from one to six and then decreasing again. When you have completed this, bring the needle up through the canvas at the top of the square at 23 and carry it right across to the opposite diagonal corner at 24. Continue diagonally across the square with decreasing stitches until you reach the corner.

Crossed stitches

Basic cross stitch is described in Chapter 4, but there are a great many variations of this simple stitch which can be used to great effect.

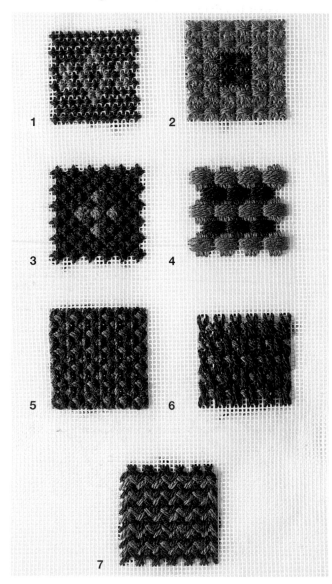

■ Crossed stitches. All stitches are worked on 12# canvas with two strands of Persian wool: **1** Upright; **2** Leviathan; **3** Double straight; **4** Broad; **5** Rice; **6** Alternating; **7** Herringbone.

Upright cross stitch

This is a very simple stitch which creates an attractive bumpy texture when used on its own and can also be used in various combinations with cross stitch.

Almost limitless colour combinations are possible: horizontal or vertical rows, diagonal lines and even different colours for horizontal and vertical stitches.

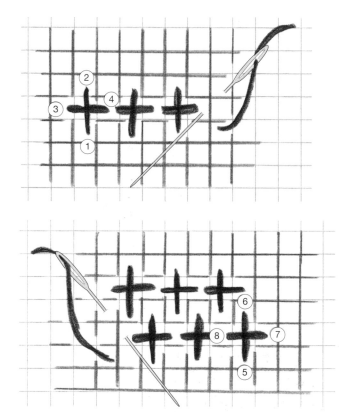

■ Upright cross stitch. Create a vertical cross following numbers 1–4. Each stitch covers two threads of canvas. The next stitch is worked in the same way and the pattern continued until the end of the row. The next row is worked back with each stitch being placed between those of the previous row, following numbers 5–8. This ensures complete coverage of the canvas.

Leviathan stitch

This is also known as Smyrna stitch or double cross stitch. It gives thick coverage of the canvas and consists of a cross stitch and a vertical cross stitch worked on top of each other.

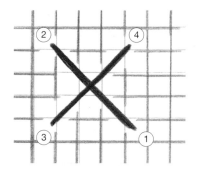

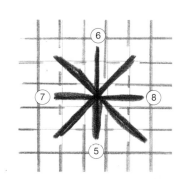

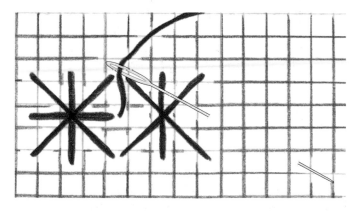

■ Leviathan stitch. The lower cross stitch is worked over four diagonal intersections following numbers 1–4. The upright cross is then worked on top (numbers 5–8). Be careful that all the crosses face the same way, otherwise the stitches will look uneven.

Double straight cross stitch

This is similar to Leviathan stitch in that it consists of a cross stitch and an upright cross stitch on top of each other but here it is the cross stitch which is on top and, whereas the resulting shape in Leviathan is a square, here it is a diamond.

As with Leviathan stitch, make sure that all the top stitches face the same way.

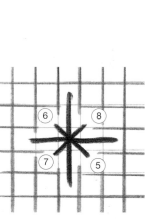

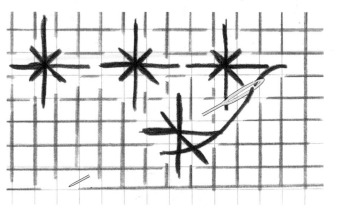

■ Double straight cross stitch. Stitch the upright cross over four threads of canvas following numbers 1–4. A small cross stitch over two diagonal intersections is then worked on top of this (5–8).

Broad cross stitch

This stitch provides an interesting pattern with an appearance similar to basket weaving. It can be used to fill in backgrounds or to produce interesting textures.

The stitch is worked over six threads of canvas and consists of three vertical stitches which lie beneath three horizontal ones. It does not matter whether you work the pattern horizontally, vertically or diagonally, provided you keep the tension of the stitches even.

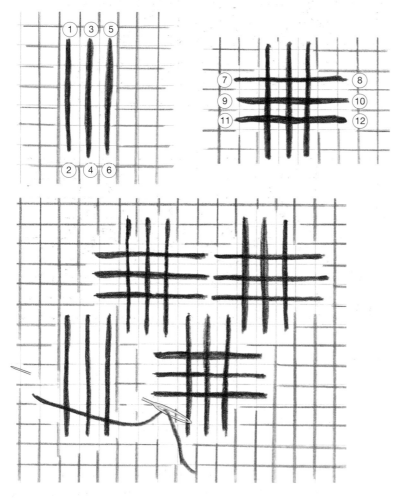

Rice stitch or crossed corners cross stitch

This provides a good thick coverage of the canvas. It consists of a diagonal cross stitch worked over an even number of canvas intersections (usually two or four). A small back stitch is then worked over each leg of the cross. If both stitches are worked in the same colour a very densely stitched pattern emerges. In the Square Picture project (pages 91–97) the back stitches are worked in a different colour, which provides interesting variations of light and dark.

If you are working the pattern in two colours, it is best to stitch all the cross stitches first and then complete the back stitches in the other colour.

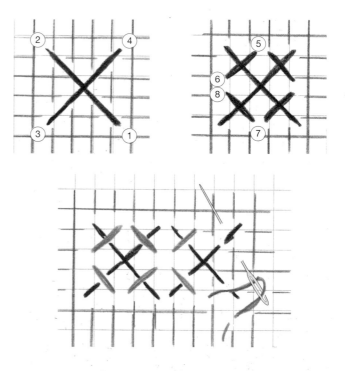

■ Broad cross stitch. First stitch the three uprights following numbers 1–6. Bring the needle up through the canvas at 7 and stitch three horizontal stitches over the top (7–12). Each of these stitches also covers six threads of canvas. The next stitch is worked directly adjacent to the first one and the rows above and below slot in between.

■ Working rice stitch. Work a diagonal cross stitch over four intersections of canvas (1–4). Then bring the wool up through the canvas at the top of the stitch (5) and work small diagonal stitches over each leg of the cross. These stitches should be half the length of the stitches forming the cross – i.e. if the cross covers four intersections, each of these stitches should cover two intersections.

Alternating cross stitch or double stitch

This stitch is made up of large and small cross stitches worked alternately across the canvas. It can be worked in one or two colours.

It is easiest to work this stitch in horizontal rows across the canvas. If you are working the pattern in two colours, you will have to complete all the large oblong crosses before stitching the small contrasting ones, but be very careful positioning the large crosses as it is easy to misplace them. This stitch can also be worked on a larger scale with the large oblong stitches covering six intersections and the small crosses covering two.

Herringbone stitch

This is a type of cross stitch which produces a pattern similar to woven or herringbone fabric.

It is worked in horizontal rows across the canvas and consists of uneven cross stitches which fit between each other.

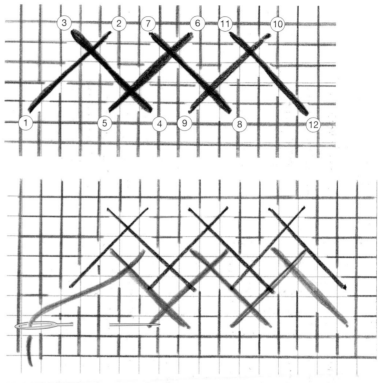

■ Above: Herringbone stitch. Bring the wool up at 1 and work a row of cross stitches following numbers 1–12. When you reach the end of the row, work the next row immediately below the first, fitting the stitches in between as shown. Be careful that the top stitches all lie facing the same way.

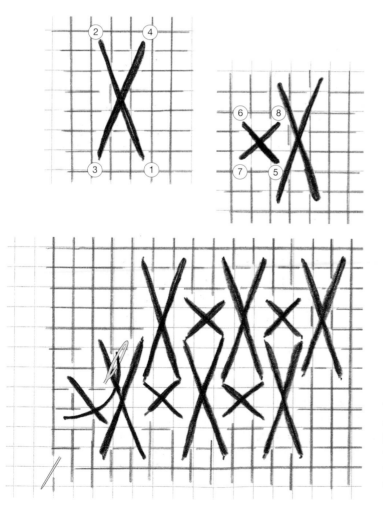

■ Left: Alternating cross stitch. Work an oblong cross stitch as shown in the diagram following numbers 1–4. Each stitch covers six diagonal intersections but is positioned so that there is only one thread of canvas between the stitches at the top and bottom. Bring the wool up through the canvas at 5 and work a small cross stitch following 5–8. Continue these alternate stitches across the row. The other rows should be worked so that they slot into each other as shown in the diagram.

Composite stitches

These stitches are all made up of a combination of stitches.

1

2

3

4

5

■ Composite stitches.
All stitches are worked on
12# canvas with two
strands of Persian wool.
1 Diamond eyelet;
2 Octagonal eyelet;
3 Rhodes;
4 Half Rhodes;
5 Leaf.

Diamond eyelet

This is made up of a series of stitches radiating out from a single central hole. When the diamond is completed it can be outlined in back stitch as this will fill in spaces on the canvas between stitches if you wish.

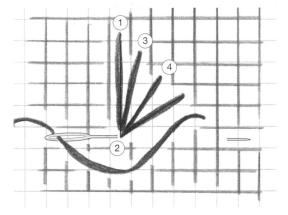

■ Diamond eyelet. Bring the wool up through the canvas at 1 and back down through 2. Then bring the wool up at 3 and back down again through 2. Each successive stitch works round the pattern but always goes back through the canvas at 2.

If you wish to alter the shape of the diamond, simply change the length of the individual stitches. The diagram below shows an octagonal stitch, which is particularly suitable for flowers.

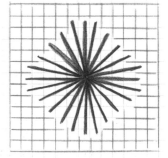

■ Octagonal eyelet stitch.

Leaf stitch

This is a fairly large stitch which can be used in a number of ways. The individual leaves can be used on their own or combined to form a pattern, in the shape of a cross or as rows of leaves.

Each leaf consists of eleven stitches. There are three parallel stitches on each side of the leaf and then five further stitches which fan out at the top.

These stitches can be worked in rows across the canvas or radiating out from a single point to form a cross.

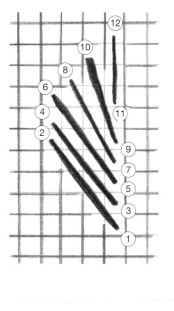 

■ Leaf stitch. Begin at the base of the leaf and bring the wool out at 1. Carry it over three threads of canvas to the left and up over four threads vertically and insert at 2. Complete the next two stitches parallel to this one following 3–6. Then stitch 7–8, which is one diagonal intersection above 6. Bring the wool up at 9, which is directly above 7, and down through 10 (again one diagonal intersection above the previous stitch 8). Come up through 11, two threads above 9, and bring down through 12 (again one diagonal intersection above 10). This completes half the leaf and the remaining stitches are worked to match down the other side, as shown.

Rhodes stitch

This stitch was invented by the British needlework designer Mary Rhodes. It consists of a square made up of diagonal stitches which all cross each other at a single central point. It can be worked in any size from three threads upwards.

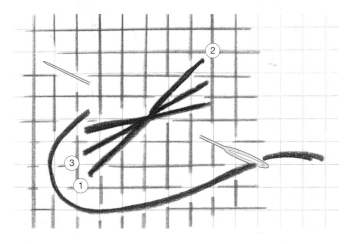

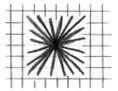

■ Rhodes stitch. Starting at the bottom corner of the square, bring the wool up at 1 and right across the square to the opposite corner at 2. Bring the wool up again at 3 and continue working round the square, ensuring all the stitches cross at the centre. If you wish, a small stitch can be worked at the centre to ensure the diagonal stitches all lie flat.

Half Rhodes stitch

A variation of this stitch can be seen in the Square Picture project. Here only half the stitch is worked and placed diagonally so the canvas is fully covered.

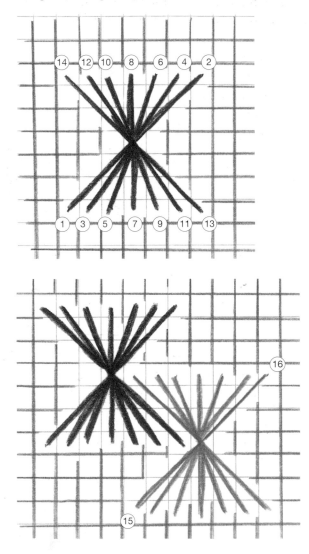

This is obviously only a small selection of the stitches which it is possible to work on canvas. In reality any stitch combination is possible, but if you are designing your own stitches or combinations of stitches always test them out on a small piece of canvas first. It is important that the canvas is covered properly and also that the stitches are suitable for the position in the pattern. Check, for example, that your outline stitches are clear and that any background pattern is not so strong that it dominates the whole piece. A pattern like the Square Picture project is particularly useful as a type of sampler as it allows you to see exactly what each stitch looks like in conjunction with others.

■ Half Rhodes stitch. As before, bring the wool up at 1 and stitch diagonally across the square to 2. Continue working the stitches across from 3 to 14, but then carry the wool down and bring it out at 15 to start the next stitch. This is three threads below 9. Take the wool back down at 16, six diagonal intersections above 15. Then continue the stitch as before.

■ Right: The square picture project.

Project 1 · Square picture

This picture is really a sampler, with each of the stitches being worked in a box outlined in tent stitch. You can either follow the stitches used here or insert any others you like. Be careful that the stitch fits into the square – you may find you need to adapt it or add extra stitches to make the pattern fit properly. This can be seen in the squares with cross stitch, rice stitch and herringbone stitch and is explained below.

Equipment needed

- 12# canvas (interlocking or mono) 14" × 14" (35 × 35 cm)
- Tapestry needle size 20
- 10" (25 cm) square picture frame
- Appleton tapestry wool in the amounts given below (these may vary if you alter the stitches):
- Pale Blue 321 one skein
- Dark Blue 749 one skein
    325 one skein
- Green 158 one skein
    851 one skein
- Turquoise 526 one skein
    525 one skein
- Pink 224 one skein
- Red 995 one skein
- Maroon 227 one skein
- Beige 981 one skein
    882 one skein
- Brown 187 one skein
    184 one skein
- Yellow 474 one skein
    851 one skein
- Charcoal 998 one hank

Stitching the design

Prepare the canvas with binding tape as described earlier. You may find it useful to use a frame for this project as many of the stitches can distort the fabric.

Counting *very carefully*, divide the canvas into squares using tent stitch over one thread of canvas, as in the diagram opposite. Each square should contain fifteen threads horizontally and vertically. Make sure all your stitches lie facing the same direction.

Then fill in the squares, following the instructions given below. Instructions for how to work each stitch are given earlier in this chapter, but some of the instructions for the straight stitches will be found in Chapter 5.

16	5	11	14	2	19	6	20
22	23	21	6	10	13	4	12
1	19	18	9	12	7	22	23
2	10	23	17	19	8	3	21
4	14	3	18	7	5	11	1
12	9	10	7	23	19	18	2
13	8	22	12	1	6	9	17
6	16	21	5	15	7	4	14

■ Stitch and colour chart for the square picture project.

■ Outline chart for the square picture project.

1. Brick stitch

The stitches here are worked over two threads of canvas using two strands of wool.

2. Straight Gobelin

The Gobelin stitches are worked over three threads of canvas. When you have completed them, stitch a row of back stitch (again over three threads) in between to cover the gaps where the Gobelin stitches join.

3. Gobelin filling stitch

Each full stitch is worked over six threads of canvas. You will need to use smaller stitches at the top and bottom to fill in the gaps.

4. Double Gobelin filling stitch

Each full stitch is worked over six threads of canvas.

5. Treble Gobelin filling stitch

Each full stitch is worked over four threads of canvas.

6. Florentine stitch

This is worked in two colours with each stitch covering four threads of canvas – see diagram.

7. Hungarian stitch

This can be worked in one or two colours. The large stitch covers four threads of canvas and each of the short stitches covers two threads – see diagram.

8. Parisian stitch

Each long stitch covers six threads of canvas and each short stitch covers two.

9. Satin stitch

This is worked in three rows, either horizontal or vertical. Each stitch covers five diagonal intersections of canvas.

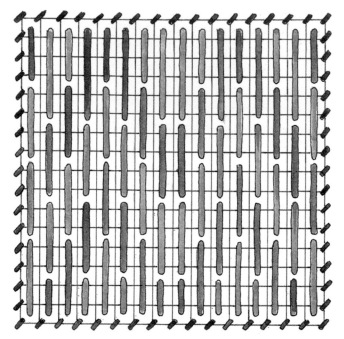

■ Patterns for the square picture project: Florentine stitch

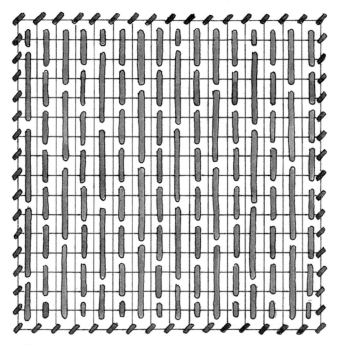

■ Patterns for the square picture project: Hungarian stitch

10. Diagonal stitch
This is worked in two colours. The stitch size graduates over two, three and four diagonal intersections of canvas – see diagram.

11. Byzantine stitch
The stitches are worked over four diagonal intersections of canvas and are stepped in groups of six stitches.

12. Jacquard stitch
This is worked in two colours. The larger stitches cover two diagonal intersections of canvas and the smaller cover one. The stitches are stepped in groups of six.

13. Chequer stitch
This is worked in two colours. The larger stitches form the corner and central squares and graduate over 1,2,3,4,5,4,3,2,1 diagonal intersections of canvas. The remaining four squares are worked in tent stitch over one diagonal intersection of canvas.

14. Scottish stitch
This is worked in two colours. The outer stitches cover two diagonal intersections of canvas and the inner dividing lines cover one. Unlike normal Scottish stitch, the infilling stitches all point inwards – see diagram. A more traditional method would be to have them all lying in the same direction.

15. Cross-cornered cushion stitch
The stitches are worked over 1,2,3,4,5,6,5,4,3,2,1 diagonal intersections of canvas. A single row of tent stitch is needed along the bottom and one vertical side to fit the pattern into the square.

16. Cross stitch
Each stitch should cover two diagonal intersections of canvas. The central row of stitches horizontally and vertically should be oblong, covering three stitches to fit the pattern into the square.

17. Double straight cross stitch
The upright crosses are worked over four threads of canvas, the upper diagonal cross stitches over two diagonal intersections.

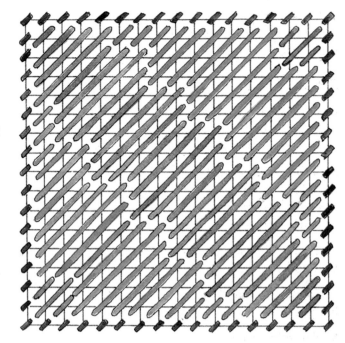

■ Patterns for the square picture project: Diagonal stitch

■ Patterns for the square picture project: Scottish stitch

18. Broad cross stitch

This is worked in two colours, with straight stitches filling in the gaps between the stitches – see diagram.

19. Rice stitch

These stitches are worked in two colours. Note the difference between the two dark blue variations: in one the darker colour is used for the small back stitches, in the other the paler colour is used.

20. Alternating cross stitch

A variation of cross stitch. Double straight cross stitch for the smaller stitches gives a thicker covering.

21. Herringbone stitch

This is worked in two colours.

22. Leaf stitch

Two leaves have been added to the single upright and a stem added at the base – see diagram.

23. Half Rhodes

This is worked in one or two colours. Six half Rhodes stitches form the pattern and the remaining blank canvas is filled with horizontal satin stitch – see diagram.

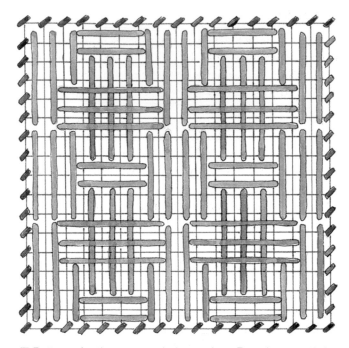

■ Patterns for the square picture project: Broad cross stitch

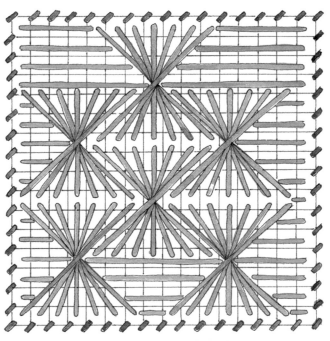

■ Patterns for the square picture project: Half Rhodes stitch

■ Patterns for the square picture project: Leaf stitch

Finishing

When you have finished all the squares, measure the canvas carefully against the picture frame you intend to use. Stitch a border in diagonal satin stitch, ensuring that the frame will slightly overlap the stitches.

Press the finished piece with a warm iron under a damp cloth and stretch if necessary, following the instructions on page 102. Fit into the picture frame, securing the canvas firmly in place with masking tape. If you do not have glass in the frame you will get a better sense of the varied textures of the piece.

Project 2 · Jewel box

This attractive jewel box is made up of jewels stitched in diamond eyelet, octagonal eyelet, Rhodes stitch and double straight cross stitch. The colours are given below but you can easily substitute your own colours; it is an ideal project for using up small scraps of wool. Be careful, however, that you use only one make of tapestry wool – for example, Appleton or DMC – and that you do not mix the types of wool – for example, crewel and Persian. If you do, the stitches will look uneven.

Equipment needed

- 14# interlocking canvas 10" × 9" (25 × 23 cm)
- Tapestry needle size 20
- Ready-made box (pad size $5\frac{1}{2}$" × $4\frac{1}{4}$"; 14 × 11 cm)
- Appleton tapestry wool in the following amounts:

Purple	325	half a skein
Yellow	554	half a skein
Gold	863	half a skein
Fuchsia	804	half a skein
Scarlet	995	half a skein
Turquoise	527	half a skein
Black	998	two skeins
Navy	748	three skeins
Red	146	half a skein
Green	645	half a skein

Working the design

Prepare the canvas with binding tape, as described earlier. Fold the canvas in quarters to find the centre and then stitch the black outline in back stitch over three threads of canvas.

Next, complete the large stitches – Rhodes, diamond eyelet and octagonal eyelet – following the colour chart. Work the double straight cross stitches in between. Fill in the blue background with brick stitch, using two strands of wool, and then measure the canvas against the box. You will probably need to work the red and green row of cashmere stitch, but it will depend on the type of box you have bought. If you still have blank canvas showing at the edge, work a row of satin stitch right round the edge in black.

Finishing

Remove the binding tape, press with a warm iron under a damp cloth and attach to the box following the manufacturer's instructions.

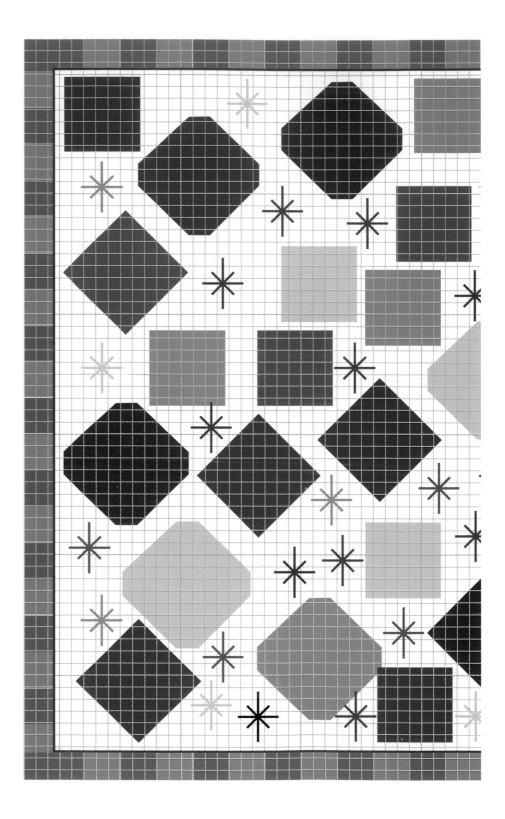

■ Chart for the
jewel box project.

Key

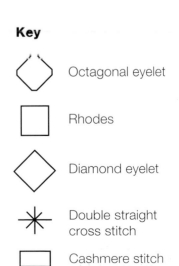

Octagonal eyelet

Rhodes

Diamond eyelet

Double straight
cross stitch

Cashmere stitch

■ Jewel box worked in needlepoint.

Finishing off

For most embroidery and cross stitch projects it is not necessary to do anything other than remove the binding tape and make up the finished article. For works on canvas it is not quite so simple!

Stretching

Occasionally the canvas will need stretching back into shape when you have finished stitching, even if you have used a frame.

Canvas is surprisingly pliable and almost all irregularities can be removed. For small pieces a board is probably best (see below) but it is also possible to tie large canvases round chairs or even doors.

The canvas should be stretched before the final finishing off rows are completed. First dampen the piece by wrapping it in a wet tea towel, being careful not to soak it. Cover a board large enough to accommodate the canvas with clean blotting paper and place the canvas face down on it. Pin the canvas to the board using rustless drawing pins or tacks, fixing it firmly 1" (2.5 cm) away from the the stitched area with pins every inch (2.5 cm). You may need to go round the board repinning several times in order to ensure that the canvas is exactly the correct shape and that it is as taut as possible; unless it is really taut the canvas will simply revert to its original shape when it is taken off the board. Leave the canvas on the board for about 48 hours and do not remove until it is completely dry as otherwise it will just return to its old shape.

For large projects you can machine stitch fabric to the canvas border and then tie the piece in place, threading fine string through the canvas every inch (2.5 cm) and then round the door, chair, table, etc.

Edging canvas

Once you have completed the pattern up to the two outer rows and, if necessary, stretched the canvas, you are ready to edge it. Remove the binding and cut away the canvas leaving 1" (2.5 cm) all round. (On canvases with 8# or larger leave 2" (5 cm).) Fold this remaining canvas over along the edge of the third row so you are left with two rows for stitches and a final half row for the border, as shown in the diagram.

Be particularly careful at the corners to ensure that the layers of canvas lie exactly under one another. It may be easier to remove a small triangle of canvas from the very corner to prevent you having to stitch through four layers of canvas.

Complete the final two rows of the pattern, stitching through both layers of canvas and making sure that the two layers line up exactly all round. This will provide a firm edge for the piece and will prevent it fraying.

The final row of half stitches will form the edge of the finished piece. If you are going to add braid, this row should be completed in the same colour as the last row of full stitches. If you are not going to add braid, the final row could be completed in three colours taken from the main piece. It is usually better not to use the same colour as the last row of stitches but three others from within the piece as this will create a better contrast between the design and the border.

Thread the needle with one of the colours and fasten it in the usual way to the reverse of the canvas. Stitch along the border with a half cross stitch, going into every third hole and making sure that the stitches face the same way as those on the main pattern. At the corners you will need to add extra stitches to ensure that the canvas is completely covered and that the stitches face in the correct direction. Continue all round the piece and then repeat using the other two colours. For a single-colour border, follow exactly the same procedure using just one colour.

The finished piece should now be pressed using a damp cloth. Always press your work face down on a soft cloth, as the direct pressure of the iron will flatten the stitches.

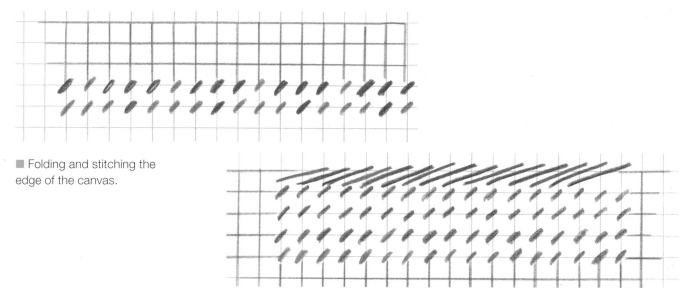

■ Folding and stitching the edge of the canvas.

Making up

Cushions

Once you have finished the border of the tapestry, iron it under a damp cloth to ensure that it is as flat as possible. Pin the backing onto the back of the tapestry, folding any excess fabric in so that the edge of the backing lies just below the final row of stitches. This ensures that it will not be visible from the front. Stitch three sides firmly and then insert the cushion. The final look of the cushion will vary according to what size of cushion pad you use. If the pad is the same size as the cover, the finished cushion will be soft and loose. For a firmer cushion you should use a cushion pad which is 2" (5 cm) larger than the cover.

Push the pad right into the corners and make sure it is lying flat before stitching the final side.

Rugs

It is not necessary to back a rug with fabric, but it is important that all the canvas edges are covered; otherwise they will fray. Trim any exposed canvas to $\frac{3}{4}$" (2 cm) and then cover it with tape, stitching it firmly to the wool on either side. Be careful that your stitches do not show through to the front of the rug.

Fringing

The character of the rug can be greatly altered by how simple or ornate its fringing is.

To calculate the quantity of fringing needed, count the number of stitches across the rug, multiply by two and then multiply by twice the length of the fringe. Remember that knotted fringes will require more. I usually fringe with knitting wool or cotton – it works out much cheaper than tapestry wool and provides an attractive contrast.

■ Fringing is a popular method of finishing off a rug.

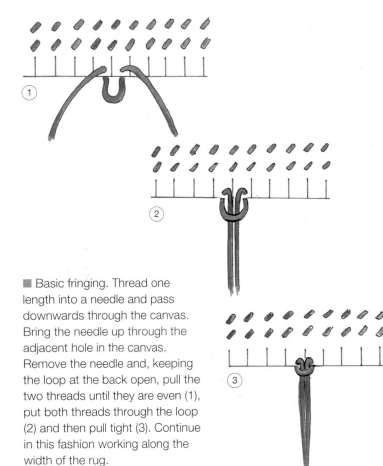

① ② ③

Try a couple of threads to work out exactly what type of fringe you want and then cut the thread into the correct lengths. Remember to allow for knots. Cut a piece of strong card with a width slightly larger than the length you need for the fringing and then wind the thread round the card. You can then cut along the edge of the card and you will have threads the right length (just over double the length of the fringe itself). The basic method of fringing is shown in the figure.

If necessary, insert extra fringes at the ends to ensure all the canvas is hidden. If you want something simple, you can now trim the ends of the fringe.

Any number of variations of fringing are possible and carpet books can be a good source of inspiration. If you are doing a complicated knotting pattern, be careful to count the number of individual fringes so that you can hide any irregularities as you go along. When doing knotted patterns, it is important to make sure that all the knots are even and face the same direction. It is best to work your way right along the rug with one row of knots and then go back and complete the next row, rather than doing each tassel individually, as this way you will notice any irregularities when it is still possible to correct them.

■ Basic fringing. Thread one length into a needle and pass downwards through the canvas. Bring the needle up through the adjacent hole in the canvas. Remove the needle and, keeping the loop at the back open, pull the two threads until they are even (1), put both threads through the loop (2) and then pull tight (3). Continue in this fashion working along the width of the rug.

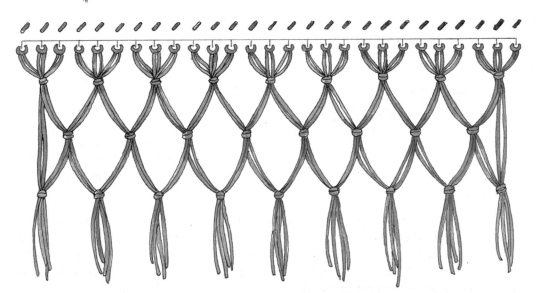

■ Fringing can be as ornate as you want to make it!

Needlecase

When you have completed the edging round the canvas, press the piece flat under a damp cloth. Stitch a cord at either end of the tapestry. These will be the ties to hold the finished case closed.

Stitch the lining in place, folding the hems over so that they lie just inside the edging. This ensures that the lining will not show from the outside. Cut two pieces of felt or blanket 1½" (3.75 cm) less than the tapestry dimension – for example, if your tapestry measures 4" × 8" (10 × 20 cm), the felt should measure 2½" × 6½" (6.25 × 16.25 cm). Use pinking shears to give an interesting finish. Fold the pages in half and stitch firmly along the spine of the case. You can attach the pages just to the lining or to both the lining and canvas, but if you do this remember that your stitches will show on the outside of the case.

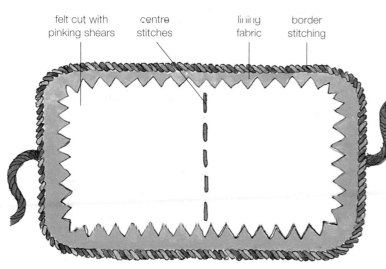

felt cut with pinking shears   centre stitches   lining fabric   border stitching

cord ties

■ Finishing the needlecase.

Book cover

(These instructions also apply to the cheque book cover.) Having completed the border, cut off any excess canvas, leaving ¾"–1"(2–2.5 cm) all round. Stitch tape over this rough edge to prevent the canvas fraying where it rubs against the book.

When the canvas is placed against the book it should be fractionally larger so that the border just overlaps the edge. Pin a piece of plain fabric to each end of the canvas to create a pocket into which the end of the book will be slotted. Fold the edges of the fabric in so that they are hidden and stitch firmly to the reverse side of the canvas. Repeat for the other end and then insert the book into the pockets.

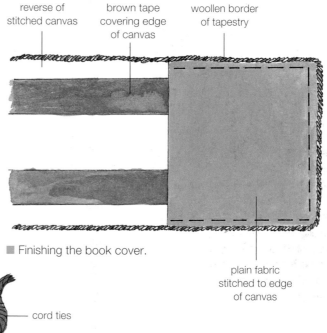

reverse of stitched canvas   brown tape covering edge of canvas   woollen border of tapestry

■ Finishing the book cover.

plain fabric stitched to edge of canvas

Pincushion

Pincushions can either be mounted onto a ready-made wooden base or backed with fabric to resemble a miniature cushion. If you are using a wooden base (available from most craft suppliers), buy the base before you stitch the canvas to ensure the two fit exactly.

If you wish to back the pincushion with fabric, follow the instructions for completing a cushion. The cushion pad inside should be filled with sand or bran. The edges of the finished cushion can then be trimmed with braid.

Drawstring bag

Remove the binding tape and press under a damp cloth with a warm iron. Fold over the excess fabric at the top and machine or hand sew three parallel rows of stitches, one near the top to create a neat edge and two further down for the braid drawstring (see diagram below).

Tuck the two ends in neatly. Then stitch the side seam, making sure the embroidered pattern lines up. Cut a circle of fabric slightly larger than the size of the base of the bag. Turn the bag inside out and pin the circular base in position. Stitch round the base and turn the bag right side out again. Finally, insert the braid.

Purse

Remove the binding tape and fold over the excess canvas, leaving one row of canvas exposed. Tack down and stitch the top and bottom as described on page xx. It is not necessary to line the purse, but the rough canvas edges must be covered or they will fray. Trim any excess canvas back to $\frac{3}{4}$" (2 cm) and then cover with binding tape, stitching it firmly to the wool on either side. Fold the bag in three as shown in the figure and tack the two sides firmly in place. Stitch over the two edges with wool, making sure all the canvas is covered.

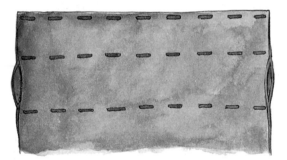

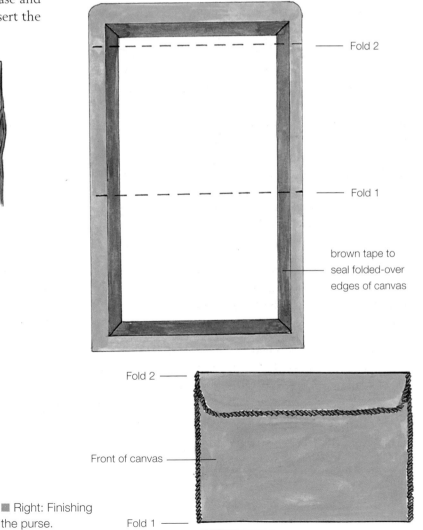

■ Finishing the drawstring bag.

■ Right: Finishing the purse.

Next make the loops to secure the bag: plait a length in three colours of wool and cut and knot two loops just large enough to go over the buttons. Stitch these loops firmly in place underneath the top flap. Finally attach the buttons on the front so that they line up with the loops.

Cleaning needlework

There is bound to come a time when your needlework needs to be cleaned and it is important that you take great care with this.

Contrary to their often delicate appearance, many embroideries are easy to wash and larger pieces can even go in a washing machine as long as you do not let them spin for too long and avoid using a tumble-dryer. Always check the colour fastness of fabric and threads. Ideally, collect small samples and immerse them in hot water – if no dye runs out into the water you are safe. If it is not possible to collect samples, dab an unobtrusive area with wet cotton wool and see if any of the colour runs. Avoid using bleach or biological powders and remember that unless it was pre-shrunk the fabric itself may well shrink.

Woollen embroideries need to be treated with slightly more care – they should be hand washed in cool water using a specialist wool detergent, otherwise the wool will shrink and cause the fabric to pucker. If in any doubt, have the piece dry cleaned.

Canvas work, such as needlepoint or Bargello, should not really be immersed in water as both the wool and canvas may shrink – and not necessarily at the same rate. Dust can be removed with the nozzle attachment on a vacuum cleaner and small areas of dirt can be sponged away. For a more major clean, or if you are in any doubt about your piece, always take it to a specialist cleaner.

■ Embroidery can be washed whereas wool must be treated with care.

8

Inspiration

Once you have mastered the technique of your chosen stitch you are ready to design your own projects. If you use a kit, the main design decisions will have been made for you, but even so you can vary the finished piece by altering the colours or even rearranging the pattern if it is printed on a chart. This can be particularly effective if you are stitching a set of pieces such as mats or cushions and chair covers.

If you are going to design your own pattern, it is most important that you ensure the stitching technique you have chosen matches the design. Many are intermixable but some embroideries would look clumsy if worked in needlepoint and other coarser-woven patterns do not translate well into embroidery. An easy way to see this is to choose a simple design, such as a flower, and work it in a variety of stitches and colour combinations. You will very soon be able to tell which designs work best with which technique.

There is no limit to the objects you can use for inspiration. Museums are good starting places but do not just look at the textiles. Wallpaper patterns often translate beautifully into stitched patterns, and pottery, porcelain and tiles can all be used.

Books are also invaluable sources. A list of useful titles is given at the end of this section. None of them deals with stitching techniques, but all contain patterns or ideas which could be worked effectively in one or more techniques.

Nature can also be a good source of inspiration – particularly when it comes to choosing colours. Try to make a record of anything you see – otherwise in six months' time, when you are trying to use the idea for a design, you may not remember all the details. If you can draw and paint, then this is a good way of recording an image, but if not, don't worry – simply take a photograph of whatever interests you.

When choosing a pattern, study the overall composition and individual elements of the original. You probably will not want to copy the design exactly but be aware of the fact that if you take only certain elements you may alter the feel of the piece. With a little practice you will easily be able to extract what you want. It may be two separate parts put together, or even just the matching of two particular colours.

It is useful to build up a collection of reference material. You can stick it in a scrapbook or album, but in many ways it is better to keep it all in a large envelope so you can rearrange the various images.

Post-cards, colour illustrations from magazines, swatches of fabric and photographs can all be useful sources of inspiration. If you see something you like, file it away, even if you cannot immediately envisage a project for it. It may be useful at a later date.

Above all, remember that your design must please *you*. If you don't like parts of a particular design, then modify it to suit your taste. Whether you are stitching your design to keep, give away as a present or even to sell, it is important that you are happy with it. The whole point of needlecraft is to enjoy the creative process of stitching, as much as to delight in the finished product.

Books of interest

The Embroiderer's Story: Thomasina Beck. David & Charles
Gardening with Silk and Gold: Thomasina Beck. David & Charles
Glorious Inspiration: Kaffe Fassett. Century
The Grammar of Ornament 1856 (and many later editions). Day & Sons
Dover Books – e.g. *Historic Textile Patterns in Full Colour*: F. Fischbank
Wallpaper and the Artist: Hapgood. Abbeville

British Museum Textile Series:
  African: Picton and Mack
  Islamic: Baker
  Nepalese: Dunsmore
  North African: Spring and Hudson
  Thai: Conway

British Museum Pattern Books:
  African Designs: Jewell
  Ancient Egyptian Designs: Wilson
  Early Celtic Designs: Stead and Hughes
  Early Medieval Designs: Wilson
  Islamic Designs: Wilson
  North American Indian Designs: Wilson
  Pacific Designs: Jewell and Lloyd

Embroidered Textiles: Sheila Paine. Thames & Hudson
Textile Designs: Meller and Elfers. Thames & Hudson

Thames & Hudson Arts and Crafts Series:
  China: Minick and Ping
  India: Cooper, Gillow and Dawson
  Mexico: Sayer
  Morocco: Jereb
  South America: Fini and Davies
  The Swat Valley: Kalter
  Thailand: Warren
  Turkestan: Kalter

Thames & Hudson Traditional Textiles Series:
  The Andes: Meisch *et al.*
  Central Asia: Harvey
  Indian: Gillow and Barnard
  Indonesian: Gillow

Places of interest

UK
- Victoria and Albert Museum, London
- William Morris Gallery, London
- Museum of Mankind, British Museum, London
- Maya, Wandsworth Bridge Road, London
- Museum of Costume, Bath
- Fitzwilliam Museum, Cambridge
- Embroiderers' Guild, Hampton Court Palace, East Molesey, Surrey
- Whitworth Art Gallery, Manchester
- Museum of Costume and Textiles, Nottingham
- Ashmolean Museum, Oxford
- Royal Museum of Scotland, Edinburgh
- Burrell Collection, Glasgow

France
- Bayeux Museum, Bayeux
- Cluny Museum, Paris
- Musée de L'Homme, Paris
- Musée des Arts Decoratifs, Paris

Italy
- Museo Nazionale, Florence
- Museo Poldi Pezzoli, Milan

Spain
- Museo Nacional de Arts Decorativas, Madrid

Portugal
- Museo Nacional de Arte Antiqua, Lisbon

Denmark
- National Museum, Copenhagen
- Kuntindustrimuseet (Decorative and Applied Arts), Copenhagen

Switzerland
- Textilmuseum, St Gallen

Netherlands
- Rijksmuseum, Amsterdam
- City Museum, Rotterdam

Germany
- Altona Museum, Hamburg
- Germanisches National Museum, Nuremburg

Hungary
- Ethnographical Museum, Budapest

Poland
- Centrale Muzeum Wlokiennictwa (Textiles), Lodz

Greece
- Benaki Museum, Athens
- Museum of Greek Folk Art, Athens

Austria
- Museum fur Volkerkunde (Ethnography), Vienna

Norway
- Norsk Folkmuseum, Oslo

Sweden
- National Museum, Stockholm
- Ethnographic Museum, Gothenburg
- Rohsska Konstlojdmuseet, Gothenburg

Russia
- State Museum of Ethnography, St Petersburg
- Applied, Decorative and Folk Art, Moscow

India
- Calico Museum of Textiles, Ahmadebad, Gujerat
- City Palace Museum, Jaipur, Rahjestan
- National Handicrafts and Handlooms Museum, Pragati Maiden, New Delhi

Taiwan
- National Palace Museum, Taipei, Taiwan

Peru
- Museo Nacional de Anthropologia y Arqueologia, Lima

Canada
- Royal Ontario Museum, Toronto
- Museum of Textiles, Toronto

USA
- Metropolitan Museum of Art, New York
- Museum of American Folk Art, New York
- National Museum of the American Indian, New York
- Brooklyn Museum of Art, Brooklyn, New York
- Fine Arts Museum of San Francisco, California
- Los Angeles County Museum of Art, California
- Textile Museum, Washington DC
- Art Institute of Chicago, Illinois
- Museum of Fine Art, Boston, Massachusetts
- Detroit Institute of Arts, Michigan
- Philadelphia Museum of Art, Pennsylvania
- National Academy of Needlearts, c/o Sharon Schuber, PO Box 17655, Anaheim Hills, California 92817

South Africa
- National Museum of Culture, Pretoria
- South African National Gallery, Cape Town

9

Computers

The accessibility of computers has increased dramatically over the last twenty years and now many people can, if they wish, make use of this technology. According to individual viewpoints, computers are regarded with emotions ranging from excitement to horror – in much the same way as machine embroidery was seen at the beginning of the twentieth century. Many stitchers fear that computers will take over the creative design process, but it is important to remember that they are simply tools in exactly the same way as a box of crayons and a pad of paper.

Computers can be useful to stitchers in two ways – firstly as a means of accessing information via the Internet and secondly as an aid to creating designs.

Accessing information

There are a vast number of web sites on the Internet relating to all types of needlecraft – in many ways the problem is finding what you want among so many choices. The best way of starting is to set aside some time, tap in a keyword (Bargello, cross stitch, embroidery, etc.) and quickly scan each suitable-looking entry. Be sure to note down accurately any entries which interest you as they may not be so easy to find again – for example, there are over 1500 sites under cross stitch alone! Many are simply companies

advertising kits for sale, but some of the smaller sites run by individuals can be more interesting – in many cases you can even correspond with the designer via the Internet. Other sites advertise or review software programs for needlecraft designs. These are extremely useful if you are thinking of buying such a program as you can get a good range of unbiased comparisons. Also you can see exactly what each program offers in the peace of your own home, rather than trying to work it out in the shop.

From out of the thousands of sites you will probably find only a few that are really useful, but even if you do not use the others they are a fascinating insight into the craft. One of the really useful sites I have discovered is Aion (www.aion.demon.co.uk). It is a UK-based cross stitch web site, but it has masses of information of interest to all needlecrafters. It offers designs by the British designer Christine-Ann Martin, as well as providing lists of suppliers, magazines and how to get hold of them, information about design, a comprehensive list of all relevant British web sites and much, much more. All the information on this site is up to date. Many of the software reviews on other sites are two or three years old and are therefore not very useful. This site also has a free pen-pals notice board which anyone can contribute to.

All the information you can gain on the Internet can be found elsewhere if you do not have access to a computer or do not want to use one. Books, libraries and telephone calls can all produce the same information and your enjoyment of stitching will not be curtailed. If, however, you do enjoy using a computer, surfing the net for needlecraft-related sites can be great fun.

Designing by computer

The other way in which computers can aid the stitcher is with software design programs. It is important to remember when choosing one of these programs that they will *not* do the designing for you – you have ultimate control over the pattern you want to stitch. Before you buy one of these programs, it is very important to do enough research to ensure that you get the one which is most suitable for you. It must have all the options you need, but not be so complicated that you are permanently bogged down in the details of how it actually works. It is here that the Internet comes in useful, and I assume that if you are considering buying a software program you are happy to use the Internet as a reference tool. Make a list of all the features you require, the capabilities of your computer and your price bracket and then carry out some research on the various sites. Two such useful sites are Fulford Software Solutions (http://member.aol.com/fulsoft) and Aion (mentioned earlier) but there are many more. Having made a shortlist of suitable programs, it is then worth actually

trying them out – most companies offer demonstration disks or exhibit at craft fairs.

A computer can be immensely useful as a tool to complete quickly the parts of needlecraft design which many people find boring – for example, patterns can be enlarged, reduced or repeated simply at the press of a button. Some programs will also be able to show you what your finished design will look like in a variety of techniques or on different fabrics and others will automatically match colours for you. All this is very useful if it is what you want. Many people (myself included) enjoy the slow design process using paper and crayons and for me half the pleasure is watching my design slowly materialise on the fabric.

Above all, you must remember that a computer is simply a piece of equipment and it is only worth considering if it makes your hobby of needlecraft easier and more enjoyable. It will not make any difference to the finished project and should not be regarded as something you *ought* to use.

■ This design could be charted by hand or computer.

Suppliers

Magazines

Individual magazines contain information on local suppliers.

UK

- John Lewis Branches
- Liberty, 210–220 Regent Street, London W1R 6AH
- WH1, 85 Pimlico Road, London SW1W 8PH
- Stable of Imagination, Syon Park Garden Centre, Brentford, Middlesex TW8 8JG
- The Embroidery Shop, 51 William Street, Edinburgh, Scotland EH3 7LW
- Wools, Wheels and Weaving, Hop Garden, Skenfrith, Abergavenny, Gwent NP7 8UF
- Lenham Needlecraft, Heath Lodge, Shurlock Row, Reading RG10 0QE (Mail Order)
- DMC Creative World, Pullman Road, Wigston, Leicestershire LE18 2DY (will advise on suppliers world-wide)
- Appleton Bros, Thames Works, Church Street, Chiswick, London W4 2PE (will advise on suppliers world-wide)

France

- Voisine, 12 Rue de L'Eglise, 92200 Neuilly Sur Seine
- Kells Corner, 28 Rue Vital, 75016 Paris
- Abacus, 20 Rue Pierre Genet, 28220 Le Mee
- DMC, 10 Avenue Ladru-Rollin, 75579 Paris Cedex 12

Italy

- Royal Blue Company, Strada Castelvecchio 40, 10024 Moncalieri (TO)
- DMC, Viale Italia 84, 1–20020, Lainate (MI)

Belgium

- DMC, 7–9 Rue de Pavillion, B 1210 Brussels

Spain

- Maidal, Principe de Vergara 82, 28006 Madrid
- DMC, Fontanella 21–3 (fl 4 and 5), E08010 Barcelona

Portugal

- DMC, Travessa da Escola, Araujo 36-A, P1100 Lisbon

Denmark

- Danish Handicraft Guild, Glentevej 70B, DK 2400 Copenhagen
- DMC, Dampfaergevej 8, Frihaven, DK 2100 Copenhagen

Switzerland

- DMC, Morgenstrasse 1, CH 9242, Obernzwit SG

Netherlands

- Benkers & Benkers, bv Dorpstraat 9–11, 5327 AR, Hurwenen

Sweden

- House of Victoriana, PO Box 8005, S-700 08, Orebo

Australia

- Penguin Threads Pty Ltd, 25/27 Izett St, Prahan, Victoria 3181
- Stadia Handicrafts, PO Box 357, Beaconsfield, NSW 2014
- DMC Needlecraft Pty Ltd, 51–56 Carrington Road, Marrickville, NSW 2204

Japan

- Yamanashi, Hemslojd 2–3–5, Kakinokizaka Meguru-Ku, Tokyo
- DMC KK, 3-7-4-203 Kuramae, Taito-ku, Tokyo 111
- Sanyei Imports, 2–64 Hirakata, Fukuju-cho, Hashima-shi, Gifu

New Zealand

- Nancys Embroidery Shop, 273 Tinakori Road, Thorndon, Wellington
- The Stitching Co, PO Box 74–269, Market Road, Auckland 5
- Warnaar Trading Co Ltd, 376 Ferry Road, PO Box 19567, Christchurch

Hong Kong

- Needleworks, A102 Villa Verde, 16 Guildford Road, The Peak

USA

- Access Commodities, PO Box 1355, Terrell, Texas 75160
- Potpourri Etc, 209 Richmond St, El Segundo, California 90245
- Potpourri Etc, 275 Church St, Chillicothe, Ohio 45601
- DMC Corporation, Port Kearny, Bldg 10, South Kearny, New Jersey 07032
- Liberty of London Inc, 108 W 39th St, New York 10018
- The Needlewoman East, 809-C W Broad St, Fall Church, Virginia 22046
- Hook n Needle, 1869 Post Road East, Westport, Connecticut 06880

Canada

- Dick and Jane, 2352 West 41st Avenue, Vancouver BC V6M 2A4

South Africa

- S.A.T.C., 43 Somerset Road, PO Box 3868, Cape Town 8000
- Needlepoint, PO Box 662, Northlands 2116, Johannesburg

Index